# Spud,
## Yesterday's
## Child

# Spud,
## Yesterday's
## Child

4-20-2019

Dan & Wendy -
Thank you for reaching out to
fellowship with me and to allow
me to share your table.
The Lord is good to give me
caring friends, who I consider
like diamonds that are unpolished,
unpublished, meant to believe in

## Padric McDuffie

un-denies love
Have a wonderful life, good
health, profitability and love for
each other.

Padric Mc Duffie

| Library of Congress Control Number: | | 2014915442 |
|---|---|---|
| ISBN: | Hardcover | 978-1-4990-6762-0 |
| | Softcover | 978-1-4990-6763-7 |
| | eBook | 978-1-4990-6761-3 |

Rev. date: 09/11/2014

**To order additional copies of this book, contact:**
Xlibris LLC
1-888-795-4274
www.Xlibris.com
Orders@Xlibris.com
611849

# CONTENTS

# DEDICATION

To the many institutionalized children who went out into the world to become parents and workers in a competitive business climate, without the benefit of having models or training in the institution that would prepare them for family structures. The give and take of relationships based on everyday living as workers, girl and boyfriends, parents, and female and male relationships within the adult world. The growing- up role models in a free society were absent from the world of foster homes and orphanages.

# AUTHOR'S NOTE

The names of people and certain places have been changed to protect the innocent and to continue the story.

# INTRODUCTION

During the 1930s and the 1940s, the United States experienced an economic depression and World War II. It became very difficult for parents with large families to support their children. As a result Foster homes and orphanages began springing up across the United Sates at a fast pace. The demand grew rapidly making these homes, more popular as a solution for these families. It is significant to point out that parents with one to five children found their independence shattered by the economic demands.

Unfortunately some parents saw an opportunity to vacate their responsibility of what seemed to be a ball and chain effect on their pleasures of living. It is also important to note that after the war, many women who became "bread winners" did not want to give up their freedom and income associated with the wartime jobs.

The journey that you will be taking as you read this book will give you a look at the real story—as seen by a boy in a real life journey through foster homes, children's homes, and orphanages—and the vain attempt of one parent who tried to hold on to her son.

As fine as the institutional residences for children may seem, in the shadows of the walls and windows of these homes were many lessons of living in a void, which may well have been unavoidable during the Depression years. These experiences are the living time for this boy. Children coming out of these institutions are naïve at best and, as such, become victims of those who would take advantage of their innocence, in many ways, by unscrupulous scoundrels.

Today we find very few of these institutions. We are indeed in an economic depression. We still have the problems facing families. Today, since there are very few (if any) institutions to house young people within family duress situations.

The grandparents' houses have become homes for the children of their children. Not without difficulty however, many of the young adults expect more from their family members. The grandparents become victims of schemes to achieve these expectations by their family's offspring. News items from across the country report this problem with accounts of elder parents and grandparents having faced severely difficult problems, and in some cases violence done by these children of the economic era downturn. Much pressure has been placed at the doorstep of many of our parents and grandparents. According to an AARP article written by Sally Abraham (2013) there are fifty-one million multiple generation homes in the United States. Many of the young adults living with parents or grandparents do try to share expenses and work around the home; however, expectations of the young, very often conflict with the established house rules of living.

# CHAPTER ONE

## EARLY YEARS

My early years were spent in a Home for Abandoned and Neglected Children. My name is Michael Johns, born August 5, 1933, according to documents provided over the years from various sources. I asked the matron about who I was and who my mom and dad were. He would never tell me. Years later when I found the home I was in I found that matron, just getting ready to retire. His name as near as I am able to determine was a Mr. Jonas. My friend for many years, Daniel Hawkins, now deceased, was a sports reporter for the Valley North News in Denver, found the address of the place when he talked to a friend of his in the welfare department. I remembered some things about the home and my trip out of the home with my new parents. When I told his friend about remembering a big sign of a train coming over the bridge, she knew right away which home I was in. We went to the home, the Home for Abandoned Children, and asked the man for information on my past. He told me the State law kept him from telling me, so it went nowhere. It would be illegal to tell me anything relating to my incarceration at the home and letters from my mom during my stay at this home. He could not even share them with me, knowing how much they would mean to me in my early, years.

He did tell me that I was brought to the home by the family services lady, and she told him I was left in the St. John Hotel in Littleton, Colorado, and they guessed my age at three to five weeks. Later my birth date was confirmed by the letters from my mother to the matron. I believe the information I was later to get later indicated that a lady and her daughter owned the hotel. They kept the baby for a week, thinking the lady would come back, but that just did not happen. The lady could not keep up with the baby's needs, and decided to contact authorities.

They called somebody from the state and turned me over to the Child Guardians of the Denver County department, who in-turn took me to the home. It has always bothered me that no person at the home or in the child services department would give me any information. It took me years to find out what home I was in. I did find out that a lady named, Helen Young and her daughter ran the St. John Hotel in Littleton, Colorado.

My earliest days of remembering my past started around three years of age when I was allowed to go out into the dirt area of the homes big yard. This was the area where the older kids got to play baseball. It was a dusty area, and every time we went in to eat lunch or dinner, we all had dirt on our faces. This was particularly true of the older boys and girls who were playing baseball and when they hit the ball and ran the bases, sometimes sliding into a base they got showered with dust. The matrons tried to get us little ones out of the dust bowl, as I heard one other older kid call the area. The matrons never let us go out onto the field by ourselves because we were too little.

One day while I was watching, a tall older girl swinging hard to hit the ball thrown at her from a boy in the middle of the field. The girl's bat came down hard on her left leg and she screamed as she fell writhing to the ground. For the minute I was standing there it hurt me so bad I cried. The girl was crying out for help, as the matron led me away back to the dormitory, but I could not get the picture of her out of my mind. I later was told that she broke her leg. I thought about that for several days as the matron was trying to get me to forget the incident. My matron was a man and he seemed old to me.

A small red-and-white bus-like car with red flashing lights and a loud screaming noise drove up and took the girl away just before we left the field.

My fun times early in my stay were when we went out into the big grassy area in the middle of the homes front property to play. This was at special times, like the Fourth of July. It was during this time that Jeremy and I got to look for four leaf clovers. Jeremy and I had so much fun looking for four leaf clovers that we began to build a good bond between us.

My matron, Mr. Jonas, told us that if we find a four leaf clover it would bring us so much luck in our lives. Jeremy and I almost in unison said, "Would it bring us a mother and a father?" Mr. Jonas' reply was "yes, that it might do so." We played several different games of marbles and tiddlywinks. We rode the merry-go-round, and got to play on the teeter-totters and swings with the matron looking over us.

It is amazing how well little ones adjust and create happiness out of situations that they are thrown into out of neglect. Our week-ends were spent staying out by the front gate fence. We wanted to see the parents come to take out their kids for the week-end. I know that Jeremy and I used to sit at the fence waiting, with a great deal of hope that one of the cars pulling up, which were rare and were mostly multicolored Taxi Cabs, came to see or get us for a day. I must say, that you could see the lines caused by tears, running down our cheeks through the dirt on our faces. We played in the dirt many games to pass the time that seemed to be nothing. A time when our lives were only the games we played. We could see the cars coming clear around the horseshoe drive connecting the buildings and the park area in the center, finally pulling up to our front. There were times when you wanted to run out and hide in the cars so you could go out. As young as we were, we talked about what it would be like us to go out for a day.

At the Fourth of July picnic we had a lot of food out on tables in the center of the lawn. *Watermelon*, they called it. They were big, round, juicy green melons with pink insides. I tasted them and immediately didn't like the taste. Mr. Jonas tried to get me to keep trying but I remember I definitely did not eat any. Everybody, including my friend Jeremy, loved to eat the Watermelon. For some unknown reason I just couldn't eat any.

Looking back at my life I think it was because everybody was eating it, and Mr. Jonas was trying so hard to get me to eat watermelon. In fact I have never liked watermelon! To this day, it may be that my aversion to this wonderful vegetable was because everybody tried to get me to eat it.

Perhaps it gave my young mind a bit of meaning amongst the crowd. Although, I have made an attempt to like watermelon since then, there has been no change of interest in the watermelon.

Our matron was a rather heavy or fat person with a balding head and he seemed very cold, looking back at him years later. He seemed very cold to us. I did find out that my mother married a man named Charles McKinney in May 1935. The research has shown that I arrived at the home December 31, 1934. After the home did quite a bit of research, and consumed many months in their search for my mother, it was an unsuccessful search.

# CHAPTER TWO

---

## WHO AM I?

Years later I was able to retrieve a copy of my adoption by Charles McKinney of Rawlins, Wyoming, married to Elizabeth Jean McKinney. The adoption paper I finally retrieved many years later from my new father Mr. McKinney. The copy was so old and faded that I did manage to get some bits of information from the document.

My name that followed me to the home was, Michael Johns, the son of one Charles and Elizabeth Jean McKinney. It looks as though the document was in the years between 1936 and 1939, as best I could determine from the faded document. I made attempts over the years later to find Russell Johns after my discovery, but with no avail. This was also the name Michael Johns left on a piece of toilet paper on the hotel bed. How cheap life is to some people.

### REUNITED WITH MOM AND NEW FATHER

My mother did apparently correspond with the matron at the home; however, I could not get any information or copies from this man at the home. The day the matron told me that my mother and father were coming to take me home I began to cry, I was so happy. I told my friend Jeremy about going home with my mom and dad and he seemed so happy for me. Jeremy waited by the Iron Fence with me until my mom arrived to pick me up. Jeremy was the same age as I. I think even toddlers know when they are wanted or belong to someone. I am sure that I was so nervous, and hoped they liked me enough to take me home with them.

When the big black car came up to stop at the Iron Fence, out stepped this beautiful redheaded woman, with big blue eyes that glistened, then a serious looking man came around from the other side of the car, they both went into the building without saying a word to me,. I thought they were here for someone else. My new stepfather, Charles McKinney, was about my mom's height, and he seemed to have such a kind face. I have always believed that my mother loved me, I just could not deal with a reason she would leave me at the Hotel.

Then out from the building comes my mother with my dad with big smiles on their faces. My mother knelt down in front of me, tears running down her pretty face, and she gave me a big hug and seemed to squeeze the life out of this little body of mine.

I loved being loved by my mom. My dad was standing with a big smile on his face, he put his hand on my head, and said, "Son, are you ready to go home? We love you very much." My dad picked up my small suitcase and we got into his black car, leaving the Iron Fence behind as we drove away.

---

I had been lectured by Mr. Jonas on how I must act politely and try not to cause my parents any problems. I think Mr. Jonas was happy to see me go. I am not sure whether he saw a problem going away or was happy for me to go with my mother and father.

## LEAVING MY FIRST HOME AND MY FIRST FRIEND

When we left the home to drive away, I looked back and saw Jeremy sitting by the fence waving at me. His face, as well as mine, usually was dusted a pale tan from the dirt on the ground in the play area. I could see the streaks from tears working their way down his cheeks as he began to cry. Jeremy was giving me what seemed to me and him, a final good-bye.

Tears began to well in my eyes. This made my heart break, and for years I remembered the look of loneliness in the eyes of my little and dear friend, Jeremy. I tried to find Jeremy years later but he had grown up and left the home for another orphanage at the tender age of nine. The home would not give me any information about Jeremy, which I thought was not right.

Mom kept looking back at me and asking if I was okay. Dad asked me if I was hungry and I said I was very hungry. We stopped at a café and I got to eat pancakes: a stack of three cakes. Boy was that a real treat for me. Well after lunch we headed for the highway and I proceeded to fall asleep.

Mom said later that I was exhausted from all the excitement and needed the sleep. To tell you the truth, I never slept the night before after hearing the good news, but I didn't want to tell my folks last night.

My dad said we were on our way to our home in the state of Wyoming. Little did my folks know that any place for home would be an exciting place for me. The feeling that I was going to be loved, sent tingles down my back, and tears of happiness swelled in to my eyes, as we slowly began to move away from the home.

# CHAPTER THREE

## MY NEW HOME

To continue on with my trip with my mother and father, the car smelled of cigarette smoke, very similar to the matron's clothes and rooms. My dad smoked in the car, I never saw mother smoke. As we approached a bridge, there was a huge sign showing a yellow diesel train, and according to my dad, coming from way back on the other side of the bridge and heading straight at us. Dad said it was an advertising sign by the Rio Grande Railroad train company to get more riders. I remembered that train and later in life that train image became a key to finding out what home I was taken to first in Denver, Colorado.

The home I just left was called the Denver Abandoned Children's Home. However, I only found out later that it was the home. I wondered how many homes I went into during the great depression of the 1930's and the war years of the 1940's. I remembered reading about the state of Wyoming later in school. I knew it was above Denver on the map. We finally arrived at New Haven, what a long trip. Everything I saw gave me an exciting feeling and I felt warm all over. A tear came rolling down my face and my mother wiped it away saying it was because I was so excited to be home.

I loved my mom and dad coming to take me home. It would have been impossible to describe what my heart and mind felt at that moment. The sun was bright and looking out the back window, it looked as though the sun was pushing back the big dark clouds to keep the sun on my window, I felt a wonderful warm feeling in my body.

My mind slowly drifted to the home I left behind, and my friend. Wondering how he is doing. I, of course, know now that for the safety and security of the inmates, as we were called by the older boys, it was necessary to protect the kids from the many problems that parents were having during the depression years. It is no wonder that children became the lowest priority for so many parents.

My mother, I later found out, told every home or acquaintance far different stories about who my real father was. He was in one conversation with the homes, a Doctor who died while practicing at a hospital, another, that my father was a drunk from Ireland who couldn't hold down a carpenter's job and headed back to his home in Ireland. And in some of the homes she said my father was dead. She also said later in my life that there were no known addresses of the step-father, which was a lie. She was well aware of his name, city and street address as well as his occupation as a railroad engineer. Mothers' lies followed me to all five homes in which I was an 'inmate'.

It was a shame that orphanages of some kind or another, in the state of Colorado, made rules that kept the homes from giving any information on the child's background to the child or any relatives who may have been able to help the child as we grew up to the age of being curious and concerned, inquiring about relatives.

It is no wonder that the kids in the home were kept in the dark, and in this darkness they found loneliness, and in the loneliness they found solace in their tears. Many cases became problem children with the guards of the inmates in these institutions. I was a perfect example of this kind of child abuse and its innate ability as a religiously oriented home for children to go through its absolute authority of "spare the rod and spoil the child" philosophy given to them by the Puritanical society in which we live.

In these homes there was no recourse to any authority of the punishments for any kind of judgment that they meted out to us. You see, they were called by God to inflict severe discipline on these whose parents solved a major problem by giving them to homes where discipline was the order of the day.

Although I remember the matrons using what they called the cat-o-nine tails, in the first home it seemed to be a strong weed type that didn't last long through the spanking but certainly had a stinging effect on the legs and back. Rulers were another choice of the day for a bit of punishment, they were used to hit the outstretched hands of the guilty party

How sad that a motherly and fatherly love was swapped for peace and freedom at their homes while placing the child on the altar of matrons who had no children or just wanted to serve God in a special way. Just a taste of real love from the guardians of the homes may have been a sweeter taste in the mouths of babes left in the desert of disciplining cactus, and a barren, desolate environment of unfruitful real love. Perhaps bitterness plays a role in the anguish of the forgotten. One was faced with the constant hours of religious fervor in later homes, with the penetrating coldness of the absence of, who we were, why we were, and what we were as individuals fearing belts of discipline that reined with such supremacy in our daily regimen. Is it no wonder that we may have become a bit bitter? The feeling of not belonging was a lonely place to be, and the thought that now I belonged was so heartwarming to me.

The next morning, my first morning in my new home, was a beautiful day. I think it is the fifth of April, but I am not really sure, my dad mentioned it in a passing conversation with my mom. In any case it is a warm spring morning and my mother made all of us a breakfast of bacon, eggs, potatoes and toast. I was still feeling the excitement of being in my bedroom, that was mine alone and I did not have to share it.

My mother was so happy to have me, and when I asked her why I was in the orphanage, she said it was just too hard to work and keep up with the needs of her baby.

I was never satisfied with that answer for some reason, but I never asked her after the second time when her Irish temper came after me for asking again after she gave me the answer before. I wonder how many thousands of kids are in the homes because it was the easiest road to follow rather than make every effort to love and care for them.

My mother met Charles McKinney in Rawlins, Wyoming, in the mid-1930s. Charles was an engineer on the railroad and took trips to Utah and various places in Wyoming. At times he would get back into New Haven late at night and when he visited his favorite bar, which was down by the

Railroad Station, he was fortunate to meet my mother. My Dad would at different times take me on short trips on the train with him. I felt so important to my father and myself on those days. What a great feeling to belong to him.

Mother worked in a house of ill repute, or as they are more often referred to it as a whorehouse. Mother worked in the whorehouse as a prostitute and often would entertain my father when he got in.

Charles McKinney had never been married and as luck would have it, he fell in love with my mother.

My mother was a beautiful Redhead, and in spite of her training as a Nurse she found the prostitute House more rewarding for a couple of reasons.

She was versed in several languages and found the money earned very gratifying and my mother was diagnosed as being a oversexed by some of her friends, however, this information was never given to Dad or myself until many years later. Charles would come off shift and throw pebbles at my mother's window, and my mother came down and took him up to her pad, so to speak. My mother would never charge Charles for her services due to an attraction for Charles, indicating a serious love that may have been somewhat true with my mother. My mother was of Irish descent, and her Red hair in no way hid the temper that was behind that hot, smart body. The bar that dad patronized as well as the house of ill repute were located just along the tracks on the north side of the Railroad Station.

My mother and Charles got married and my mother had previously told Charles she had a son, named Michael Johns, whose father, Russell Johns, had fallen ill during an operation, and died of pneumonia. When her Doctor Husband passed on she immediately left the St. John Hotel in Littleton, Colorado, and left her son on the bed with a name tag of Michael Johns. The mother and daughter that were taking care of the hotel kept the baby for 2 weeks thinking the mother would return for the baby. Charles wanted to get the baby, which he did.

## MY DAD

The baby was placed in the Home for Abandoned Children in Denver, Colorado. Charles and my mom got married and the first thing Charles wanted to do was to go and get the baby. The State of Colorado and the County of Denver were not receptive to placing the baby back in the arms of his mother,

Charles had to go through several hoops, and the judge wanted him to adopt the baby before they would consider releasing the child to their custody. My new name became Michael McKinney. My Dad was as proud as a peacock of his new son. My new Dad was such a loving father to me. He did take me down to the newspaper store every Tuesday with him to get cigarettes and five news magazines. My interest in reading the news, I am sure, came from my father. I was one happy camper as I grew in his custody. He opened a whole world for me to see. When we were returning to the house from the trip to the store, he would always stop by his favorite bar for a bourbon-and-soda drink or a straight Christian Brothers Brandy. Brandy was his favorite drink. My home life was one that would be the envy of many kids then and now. My Dad took time with me because he loved me, not because it was a duty of fatherhood.

My dad would take off to run the trains and some days he would not come home until real late from his trips, or at times he was gone a couple of days.

My dad was a wonderful father to me, something I didn't imagine I could have received from living away from the orphanages. My mom's baked bread spoiled me for the rest of my life on what I really liked in bread. When I went to school, my mom knew that I loved her fresh baked bread and would come running home to get it. She also baked great pies. I liked her cherry and apple pies—they were fresh, and hot as well, after just coming out of the oven. But there was nothing like her homemade bread. I think I am still addicted to homemade bread.

You could smell the aroma of the fresh baked bread all the way home from school. Mom knew this was a way to get me home every day as soon as school was out.

New Haven wasn't a big town but it was heaven to me. My dad used to take me by the hand and walk down town to the news/tobacco store. The distance seemed so long to me but in my dad's hand, it was all right. My dad would pick up the news magazines—*US News*, *Time*, and *Newsweek*—two other magazines and two cartons of Lucky Strike cigarettes, and off we would go heading home. However, dad always took a route that included the street running along by the railroad station, which was a pretty long red brick building. Across the street from the railroad station were bars and houses that ladies used for business. We would proceed to a local favorite bar of my dad's and we went in to the bar. The bar seemed old and had a musty smell, I guess from the beer sold there and probably spilled there a few times it had this certain smell. I was with my dad and everything was just fine. He introduced me to many of his friends since the first day I went with him to the News/Tobacco Store. My Dad would read every one of those magazines from cover to cover every week.

He talked to me about some subjects we were studying in school, especially the articles that were relative to what the magazines were writing about. He made me hungry for information at a young age. I carried that hunger for knowledge the rest my life's journey.

He let me read the magazines along beside him in the evening, even though he knew I was looking at the pictures. But every once and *awhile* I would ask him a question, and he would give me an intelligent answer, this kept me interested in the news, up to the present. My dad was a smart man streetwise and in the academics.

Today was a special day, and as usual my dad sat at the bar and had me sit up at the bar with him.

The bartender and my dad have known each other for years. My dad would order a beer and a shot of whiskey, and for me, he ordered a tall Coke. I felt so important there with my dad. After we left the bar where my dad had such a good time, and I did as well, dad took my hand, and we started for home. I remember several times when we were at the bar, and I asked my Dad why I couldn't have what he had at the bar. He always said, "When you grow older, I will let you have what I have."

On we went towards home. We passed the Catholic church where he said I was baptized. When I asked him what being baptized meant, he said he and my mother were both

Catholics and it would "lock in a place in heaven for him, my mom, and me".

When we got to Pine Street, I knew we were home. Being home meant that there would be fresh bread and a piece of pie for us. Mom worked as a nurse during the days that dad was off work. I never talked with my mom about her work. She was so pretty in her white uniform, white cap, and a blue-and-red cape that hung around her shoulders.

Depending on what time we got back from the news store, if it was early in the afternoon or morning, I got to go out and play.

My mom took me downtown to a store where they sold roller skates. Now let me tell you, this was a royal treat for me. I had tears welling in my eyes, and asked me why I was crying. I told her it was so exciting to me to have something like this that was my own, and nobody else would have this pair of skates.

## MAKING FRIEND

She worked with me, and taught me how to skate I became quite good, and I began to go around our block. It was so much fun. I met a little girl. She said she was five. Her name was Lewellyn, and this girl could skate. She was out skating me when we first met, but I managed to get up to her speed. I took her home to meet my parents and, of course, have some of Mom's pies. Lewellyn and I became the best of friends, and we got permission to go further around three blocks when we were skating. The following week, I met her dad who worked at the prison at night, but was always home during the day. He was an older man, but he was sure nice to us kids. I never met her mother.

Later on in our friendship, she told me that her mother had passed away at an early age. Her dad never remarried. When I was around Lewellyn's father in their home, he seemed so good to his daughter and to me. I would never believe that a father like him would put his daughter into a home like the one I was in and had been in for years. I was going to get to go to school this year, and was I excited. Lewellyn was also going to school this year. The grade school was an old wooden building painted yellow. It also had an outside door down to the cellar.

They had a lot of coal down in the cellar because it was used for heating the school house. Both Lewellyn and I were in the first grade, and so we could study together and always walk home from school.

We met a lot of new students and I was a bit shaky at first. I guess it was because it was new to me. The teachers were very interested in my learning ability, as they were in all of the students' learning abilities. Lewellyn knew some of the kids because of kindergarten, so I became more familiar with more students.

According to the teacher and the principal, I was a troublemaker and seemed to get into fights with some of the boys from the south side of the tracks. The students lived over on the other side of the railroad station, beyond the railroad tracks. They all knew each other, and it was easy to tease me, with my freckles and fiery red hair and a chunky build. I went home a few times with bruises and skinned places on my face and arms often.

I remember one time when one of the boys was teasing Lewellyn, and she couldn't get them to leave her alone. The principal or teachers would talk to them, but when they were out of sight, they were right back at it. I jumped into the middle of this teasing going on and began defending my good friend. Needless to say, the bigger boys got the best of me. My Mother, when she saw me come home one day with so many bruises and a little blood, got so mad she unleashed a verbal assault on the principal. I felt sorry for the principal because he tried to step in to calm the bigger boys who quickly apologized in front of the teachers and principal. This lasted until the next recess or lunchtime, and they were back at it again.

My mother told me to keep it away from my dad because he was a Golden Glove boxer and fought a lot in his younger days. My mom finally had to tell my dad, who immediately went down to a sporting goods store and bought a fast bag. Dad called it a speed bag and also a heavy big bag.

He hung the bag in the basement and began training me on the art of fighting. He said I learned very fast and to only use these skills when necessary. Well, my friend loved coming down to our basement to watch me work out on the bags. I transferred all of my training from my dad to the school yard. I soon did not have much trouble from the boys across the tracks,

However, now the teachers were after me for hurting the boys from across the tracks. I fought so much in second grade that they held me back. This year was so different for me in this school. I won the singing contest at our school and ending the year liking a set of blond haired twins. I defended one of them on one occasion which got me sent home for two days.

The music teacher motivated me to enter the contest, and as a result, I have loved music so much all my life. I also excelled in sports, and it tied into my training at home.

I remember one fine day, when I was showing Lewellyn my ability to climb trees, I fell. I was up about thirty feet, according to my father, and when I fell, I was knocked out, which brought my mother and dad home quickly. A neighbor, Mrs. Worley, came out of her house and quickly called the ambulance. The authorities were able to get hold of my parents, and they came to the hospital.

I recovered that night, and the hospital let my parents take me home. They were very concerned that I might have broken some bones, but they said I was ok.

My mother and Father were wonderful at Christmas time. They showered me with wonderful presents, one of which was a real Christmas tree with presents underneath.

Last Christmas, my dad bought me a real Lionel Electric Train. Boy, was I excited. Mom always bought me real nice clothes, and one teacher commented to me that I was always dressed very nice.

This did change a bit when I got into fights. I loved my mother and father so much. I was worth something, and dad made sure I believed in myself and in them.

My dad told me a story about when he was young in his late teen years. He didn't find good jobs and was always short of money and food. He went down to the city park where all of the older men used to play chess. My Dad said he learned the game of chess and began beating the men down at the park. He said he earned eating money.

He said he always got his lunch paid for by these fella's, and very often, some extra money for other things. Dad said when he went to work on the Pacific Limited Railroad, he gave up playing down at the park. I played chess with my dad when I met him later in life, and he beat me every time. We played by phone for a while, but soon quit that. Perhaps, remembering this about my dad kept me on top of a work ethic that has followed me all my life.

I was having such a wonderful life with my parents. I honestly felt I belonged to them and that I would spend the rest of my life with them. Mom and dad were having trouble for some reason. At first I thought it was because I was such a problem at school and at home. On one of our trips to the news store, to get magazines and tobacco, I ask my dad if I was causing him and to get into arguments. He said, "No, son, sometimes adults don't see eye to eye on everything and it makes for disagreements." When we stopped at the bar to say hi to many of his friends, the questions I asked of him seem to be not important now. They served my dad his usual beer and whiskey, and he was going to get me a Coke when I popped up and said, "Dad, why can't I have what you have?" —a question I had asked each time we came to this bar.

He looked at me and then at Tony the bartender, and said, "Tony, I need to get you to give him a small glass of beer."

My dad knew it would make me sick, but Tony obliged my father and gave me a small glass of beer. I was one proud puppy of a son, and as my dad and others looked on, I picked up the glass the way my dad does and took a big drink of the beer. I immediately became sick and had to throw up in the bathroom. My dad took me into the bathroom quickly, knowing that I was sick. I never wanted to drink beer ever again until I was a junior in College. I could not even stand the smell of beer. It taught me a lesson I am sure—certainly not one that should be given to other kids who are as curious as was I.

Little did I know that my mom was working at our house. She must have done this when I was in school during the day. My dad later told me that she was entertaining men during the day while he was on long trips. According to my dad, a neighbor of ours was retired at that time and watched as my mother had several male visitors during the days when dad was on the road. Dad took a day or two off and didn't tell.

He stayed over at the neighbors' house and watched the parade of males that went into his home. My dad said that there was a green vase that always sat on the mantle of the fireplace. My mother would put the green vase on the front window with a rose in the vase on days when she was open for business.

This was the reason my mom and dad yelled so much at each other. I thought at one time it was over me, but they told me it was not. One fine sunny day when I came home with my friend, Lewellyn, my mother said I was going to live with a Mexican family on the other side of the train tracks for a month.

She said she and Dad needed some time to work some things out. I learned to eat Mexican food, especially tortillas with beans rolled up in them. I liked them all my life from that experience, and especially the beans. They were nice people to be with, but I began to feel all alone again, a feeling I did not want to repeat. These folks wouldn't tell me anything about my situation.

My folks brought me home again, and my Dad said that my mom and I were going for a two week trip to see her relatives. I felt an empty body surrounding my day, and I became very upset and alone.

My dad tried to calm me down, but the tears just came pouring out and my heart was broken. I loved being a part of these two people that were my parents. My mother told me we were going to see her family for a couple of weeks, but I didn't want to leave my dad behind. I had a hard time packing to leave, tears were clouding my vision, and my heart felt like it was broken. I looked at my dad as we were going on the train, and I know I saw a little stream of tears rolling down his wrinkled suntanned face. I gave my dad the biggest and best hug I could do as we got on the train. Mom found the seats right away, and I ask her if I could stand on the platform at the rear of the last car to watch and wave at my dad.

The conductor said it would be all right as long as my mother was there with me and to make sure to hold onto the rail that went around this little platform at the back end of the rain.

My dad stood waving, and I saw him wave. His eyes seemed to just hold me in his focus until I was out of sight as I stood there and waved at him. I could barely make him out through the torrent of tears running down all sides of my face. Looking at my dad waving was like looking through the windshield of a car when it was down pouring rain. On top of this my heart, was hurting so much.

I could barely make him out as we began to move away from the station. My mother stood behind me, lightly holding on to my coat. I was sad and didn't want to talk to anybody, and in a way, I felt my mother was responsible because she used to scream a lot at me and my father. My mother never changed that raging personality. I felt it much later on when I was staying at one time with my mother in a hotel one time. We stopped at a town called Turlough, Wyoming. We took a cab to an orphanage called St. Dominic. It is a beautiful spring day out, and the sun felt warm on my shoulders. The cab let us off in front of the home front gate which opened to a long walk, leading up to a big brick building.

# CHAPTER FOUR

## FADING PICTURE OF DAD

Sometimes I feel like dates and time are tunnels through which I must travel, always wondering what is on the other side, and I must travel without choice or direction as we began walking down the walk I felt that life was without meaning. I guess I felt that my dad gave so much meaning to my life, and I lost the touch of his mind and hand as we walked along. I had a hard time wondering why if we were going on a vacation, why we stopped here at this orphanage.

My mother seemed to get me out of my thoughts when she grabbed my arm and said, "Let's go, Bobby!" There were nice people waiting just ahead of us. A father and a sister came out to greet us and took us inside. The priest name was Father Jones, and inside he introduced us to another priest, a Father George.

Mother had lectured me on being nice to these people, while the heavy suitcase kept banging against my leg, and it was getting me tired and sore in the elbow and hip.

My mother told me that I would only be here for a few days, maybe three weeks. Father Jones agreed with my mother on time, so I thought we would be going home to New Haven in a few days—how wrong I was to believe this story. A lady in an office took my mother aside to make out what appeared to be papers of some kind. While mother was doing this, Father Jones sat me down and told me what the home was like and that I would like it here with all of the other boys with which to play.

Another Father came into the room, and Father Jones introduced him as Father George. He had a warm smile on his face, and his eyes were a soft brown that seemed to smile right along with his smile. Father George was the Headmaster. He sat down beside me and began telling me all the good things that went on at the home.

He seemed gentle concerned that I should be happy. While at the time, my heart was breaking.

I told him I had a father in New Haven, but he seemed to think it was not the truth. I think my mother told him what so often she told others—that my father passed away when I was very young. Father George put his arm around my shoulder and began walking me through the building. It seemed by the sound of this that he had been here many times before. The building had very high ceilings, and the floor was composed of square rocks—all the same sizes, about a foot square. Father George talked to me like my dad, and that made me feel more comfortable. He took me up this huge staircase to my dorm.

There must have been fifty boys staying in this room. It was so large and with so many beds and dresser drawers. I was still hanging onto my suitcase, and when we arrived in this dorm, Father George showed me where to put my clothes and where the restrooms were. The headmaster said he must go now and left me standing next to a bed which he said was mine. I walked over by the window and looked out at the gate which my mother was just walking through. I began to cry and it seemed I was all alone again without my dad and mom. Mom didn't say good-bye or give me a hug. It was like she was in a hurry to get out of here. The cab picking her up became a big blur through my tears, and I felt forsaken by my mom and my dad.

I heard a lot of noise, and down the hall, a bunch of boys came. I quickly dried my eyes as best I could. I was still standing by the window when a voice behind me said, "Are you the new boy?" and I said yes without turning around.

The voice said, "Welcome to the prison dorm. I hope you will like it here." I turned to see a colored boy, his teeth white like pearls, the boy I saw out on the lawn playing when I was looking out on the way up the long walk. By this time my eyes were somewhat dry, but red, and my nose had stopped running. I turned around to see. His name was Brandon, and I told him my name was Michael McKinney. Brandon helped me put my clothes in the drawers and then showed me the bathroom where we had to wash up for lunch, which is served exactly at twelve o'clock noon on the dot. We got into a water fight in the bathroom before we went down to eat. Brandon introduced me to other boys, but I could not remember their names. Down at the table, everyone stood by a prearranged place setting and said a short prayer for the food.

After the prayers, it was like a gun went off to start a race. Everyone was pushing, shoving, and knocking each other to get to the food first. The food was served in large dishes, so the boys took what they wanted to eat. The kitchen staff kept the bowls and plates full so we wouldn't starve. You would think it was the last time for them to eat, the way they were going after the food. It didn't take me long to figure out that I wanted to be in the first bunch as well. I guess the food was fresh and tasty then.

This home was similar to the home I was in before I met my new dad. Everything was run by the clock and the whistle. Brandon and I walked out after lunch talking about when we were to go to bed and things like that.

I liked Brandon! He wasn't cocky, mean and sloppy like boys I knew in school in New Haven. I like Brandon a lot. Brandon got to see his mother every Sunday afternoon. I thought that was nice.

He had been here for three years. I told him my story and that I was going to be leaving in three weeks. When Brandon was talking about his folks his voice sounded hollow, and I could tell he was not happy here at the home.

As we walked outside, I noticed the sun setting in the western sky over New Haven and the mountains—well, really, the mountains were really like rolling hills, like a wrinkled blanket covering on the ground.

We ate at six, so it must be seven o'clock by now. The time just whizzed by today. I think Brandon being there kept me from feeling the loss of my parents. The evening sky was so pretty with the clouds as they reflected the orange and purple colors from the sun that were bouncing off them. The clouds were lined up in levels as though some giant were spreading frosting over glass steps under which I was standing, and I was underneath watching. Off to the north, I noticed one small cloud, all alone and moving slowly toward the big clouds. It was so cute to watch. Brandon startled me when he asked me to go and play the rings with him, something I had never done before. Jim was so good at the rings, and I was trying hard to learn from him. But I was getting so tired I suggested we walk over the grounds, which were ever so big, and see if we could catch a horny toad. Toads go in about dusk, but sometimes, I would catch one going back to their holes.

Darkness was setting in fast and as we started to head for the house, the whistle blew, and we were off to wash up and jump into bed.

After we were in bed and the lights were out, I began thinking of my warm room at home and Mom and Dad coming in to say good-night. I missed the smell of Dads' cigarettes and my mom's perfume.

Tears began swelling in my eyes, and when I began sniffing, I put my head into my pillow so no one could hear me. After a while, I stopped and turned over on my back to look at the ceiling, which was white with little designs that looked like a chain-link fence going across the room. And there were little people working carrying bricks from one pile to another and back again. They never seemed to finish or get tired. Their hard work made me tired, and before long, I was working with them. As I closed my eyes to sleep, I was carrying bricks from one pile to another. Yes, that was my first day, but now many weeks later, the Iron gate looks more like bars on the windows of a prison and the big yard is not so big but very small.

Brandon and Herald my nice friends, are still here, but we don't play together much anymore, and that is my fault. I am still thinking, *maybe Dad will come for me*. The grass is not so green and soft for me but rough, bare and brown. The whistles from the trains don't blow for me anymore like they used to when Dad drove the trains, for I don't need them. The setting sun has a redundancy filled with fear and doubting in its fading shadows that seem to claw their way across a partly cloudy evening sky.

Mother hasn't come back to get me, and the black robed wardens won't let me go away. Every Sunday, I sit by the big window upstairs, watching parents come for their children, but see none coming to claim me.

Mondays, Tuesdays, Wednesdays, Thursdays, Fridays, and Saturdays, I sit by the gate and look for my mom and dad. Many cabs come by, but none with my name on them,

I write to my mom and dad to the sheriff's department in New Haven, Wyoming, but never hear back. I heard my mother tell the fathers that since my father died, I have been under the illusion that he can still find him, and this exercise makes me lonelier as time passes on. That I shouldn't send out letters to my father who is not there.

## OFF TO ANOTHER NEW HOME

As I was sitting in my usual waiting spot by the upstairs window, I saw a taxicab pull up to the outside gate, and I was so excited my heart was pumping fast as I ran down the stairs to go and meet my mom. I just knew she would be in that taxicab. When I got downstairs and ran to the front door, I saw my mother walking up the long white sidewalk.

It seemed that she was walking fast because the leaves along the walkway kept blowing around her feet

I was right, and when I saw my mother coming down the walk to get me, I was so excited that I began running and crying toward her. I seemed to be overwhelmed with joy.

Mom held out her arms to hold me, and the perfume that she wore was such a welcomed smell as I pushed my face against her tummy and held on for dear life so as not to lose her. Even though I was crying for joy, I never lost sight of her coming up the walk. I loved my mother. When she hugged me I could smell her perfume, that she always wore, and I became even more excited.

After some conversation with the fathers, she asked me to go get my clothes.

The Sister Jane went upstairs with me and packed my clothes in a big paper bag. I ran down the stairs, and seeing my two friends standing by the door, I said good-bye as tears began rolling down my cheeks and dropping onto my shirt.

I was both happy and sad. I learned later in the orphanages that my friends were really my only possession, and I was losing two more friends in my journey to some place. Mom said, "Go say good-bye to your friends, and then we will leave." Mom wanted me to say thank you to the fathers and sisters, and then we left for the taxicab that was still waiting by the gate. I got to sit next to the window and see the antelopes run along in the fields.

I really missed my father he was a giving person that loved me unselfishly and with an unconditional love. The people at this home tried to quiet my feelings and help me adjust to the new home. The father at the home said I was disrupting the other children staying in the home.

Every time I asked my mother about my dad, she would tell me it would be awhile before I could see him. His work would keep him away. After awhile, I stopped asking because it was making her angry, and I knew what that meant.

Every time we stopped to take on more people, we got to go into the building for the restroom. My mother would take me into the women's restrooms with her, and it was very embarrassing to me.

She made me stand against the wall while women were coming in and out. She said it was to keep other people from hurting me. I hated that time when I stood against the wall by the door. Mother did what she had to do.

She also had me go into a stall and do my thing. It was so hard for me to be there in that women's restroom. I did get tired of women patting me on the head and saying, "You are such a good boy." I couldn't help but wonder how they knew. Our journey took us through Cheyenne and then we came to Denver, in Colorado. The Denver bus stop was a big place, with lots of people. My mother held onto me real tightly, and I was scared of all of these people. Mother got something to eat from a machine—a candy bar and some potato chips that tasted good to me. We did go into the ladies room again then we sat in the bus depot on a very hard bench. Mom started talking with some man, and after a while, he stood up and gave my mother some money.

She went to a window in the depot and got two tickets to Colorado Springs.

Mom came back to the man and promised him she would send him back his money as soon as she could. I don't know if she ever paid the man back for his loan. Thinking back, she told me so many lie I think she was consistent in her habit of lying.

Off we went to Colorado Springs on the bus. The road was more beautiful than the trip across Wyoming. There were lots of trees and mountains that I got to see out our window. I spotted a big deer and a little deer running through the trees and out into the fields. Boy, was it beautiful to watch them and see how free they were running among the trees. I watched them until we passed by them on the road. In a way, I thought it would be great to feel as free as they look. I was tired and fell asleep with my head on Mom's shoulder. Mom woke me up when we got to Colorado Springs. Again the bus depot was a big and busy place. A lady came to pick us up. Her name was Lorraine. As near as I could tell, this woman was of my mother's side of the family tree, and we stayed at their house one night.

The next day mother bought some more tickets, and away we went to Pueblo, Colorado. I went to sleep again, and I was awakened by the sudden stop. We got off of the bus, and one of those yellow cars with the sign on the top picked us up and we went to a home where there were a lot of other kids.

We went to a Catholic school. I believe this was called Saint Julia's School. I don't remember much about it other than it was the school to which we all went. The class that

I was in was so much fun. The sister set up wires across the top of the room, and each student had a wire assigned to them.

On the wire were little race cars. The cars were moved as we went through the assignments. If you went through your assignments rapidly, your car was moved up on the wire.

I worked hard and had my car moved all the way to the end. The teacher let me read a book on Huckleberry Finn. I became bored and decided to make spit balls to shoot around the room. I shot one at the sister's dress skirt, and some of the kids laughed a bit. I could see the teacher did not feel the spit ball I shot so I decided to do it some more. I was ok for a short time, but my aim was off. And the sister bent over to pick up something, and my spit ball hit her under the cardboard top. Well, it was over for me, and she grabbed my ear and twisted it hard while I had my hands spanked with a ruler. Boy, I was in trouble! The sister took me down to the father-principal's office—not a fun journey. I got the cat of nine tails across my backside, and I thought I was going to die. The next day, my mother came to pick me up and take me out of this home. I don't know if the home called my mother and told her to get me out of the home or my mom made that decision based upon reports from the temporary home.

Mom took me over to a home which looked awful big to me. It was red bricked and white trimmed, and it looked three-stories high. The home was called the McDermit Home for Children. When we walked through the door into the lower hallway—which, I might add, was huge and seemed to reach the sky.

A heavy set woman with a voice to match her size came out to greet us. Mom had made arrangements before our arrival, and the lady mentioned her earlier conversation and began to discuss my situation with the lady. She told Miss Wesley I was without a father and that he died years before. He was, according to my mother, a medical doctor and died from a disease contracted during an operation. In any case, I had no father, according to my mother; however, I knew better and began to say so when my mom shut me up very abruptly. She also said that I was given to illusions about my father and it seemed at times to make me more despondent.

Miss Wesley called in a matron to take me and my suitcase up to the boys' dorm. My mom was going to do some paper work with Miss Wesley, and sent me off with the matron that Miss Wesley had assigned to me. Just before we started up the stairs, a boy was hanging over the upper portion of the stairway, talking to this matron. All of a sudden he looked at me and called me Spud—a name that made me angry. I looked him in the face and was going to remember it for sure. He made me so mad and angry because I never liked being called different names, especially by someone I didn't know. I had been there before with other names in other places and already planned to meet with that boy, even though he looked older and taller than I. After we went into the room and found my drawers and bed, I asked the matron if I could go down and see my mother before she left.

Mom said her good-bye to me, hugged me, and kissed me on the cheek, and said she loved me and went out the door after Miss Wesley assured her that I would be a happy boy and that the home would take care of me for her.

After Mom left in the taxicab, Miss Wesley took me into her office and began telling me the rules and regulations that I would have to follow here at the home. I could not hold back my tears as I watched her going away; and in my heart, I knew I was not going to see her again.

Miss Wesley gave me some tissues to dry my tears, but they were like the water after the dam breaks—I just couldn't stop crying. Miss Wesley finally got me calmed down and began again to tell me my rights and wrongs within the rules of the home.

I should get used to my mom leaving me, but she was all I could hang on to because we left my father back in Wyoming. I felt, at times, it was like grabbing at the low white clouds that just faded away from me. My Dad never did get a hold of us. I guess he didn't want me because I was a problem, or he just didn't like me anymore, and that made me very sad.

Miss Wesley tried to cheer me up as she put her heavy arm around my shoulders and walked me up to the second floor to the little boys' dorm. Her arm was so heavy it seemed to add weight to my body as we climbed the stairs.

This dorm was a huge room and divided by about a four-foot partition, running long wise down the middle of the room. The big boys were on the left as you come into the room from downstairs, which would be the south side, and the little boys' room was on the right facing the street, and it was on the north side.

There were eight beds on each side of the partition. Miss Wesley introduced me to the matron that would be my daily and fulltime matron. Her name was Miss Holquist.

She was somewhat tall with graying black hair, and she wore glasses. You could smell cigarettes on her when she put her arms around me and said I would be fine at this home. Miss Holquist had her own room and restroom facility, a small apartment-like unit.

The oldest boy in the home at that time was Howard Wolker. He was fifteen or sixteen; I wasn't quite sure. I only knew that from some of the old-timer kids that had been there for some time. He had special privileges with Miss Holquist. I think he was her favorite boy. Howard would get to go into Miss Holquist's room after we were all in our beds. The door to Miss Holquist's room stayed closed. You could see a thin line of light at the bottom of the door—at least until I went to sleep. I think they played cards or something.

I never got a reply from Howard when I asked what they did so late at night. In fact, Howard got mad at me for asking and told me to mind my own business and to keep my mouth shut. I thought on several occasions he was going to beat me up, but he never did.

One of the things I remember most was that they didn't try to persuade you to go to any certain church—that was a nice thing. My mother told them I was baptized a Catholic, so every Sunday morning, I was given a quarter to put into the church collection at the local Catholic church. I learned from some of the other boys that the Upstage Theater showed cartoons on Sunday morning between ten and twelve noon, and that we could go there and get a bag of popcorn while we watched the cartoons, all for twenty-five cents.

We would walk in the front door of the church and do the water thing, and then go out the side door and on to the theater. That was a great idea, and it sure was worth looking forward to church on Sunday morning. The Upstage Theater was down the street on Abriendo Ave. The home had a carriage house out to the left and to the rear of the home. According to one of the boys, this was at one time an estate for a wealthy family who donated it to the home for children. I don't know what they used it for, but one of the boys said it was for some of the people who worked at the home. Beyond the home proper and to the right of the carriage house existed a big vacant lot, and the kids often played different games out there such as baseball and speedball. This lot ran all the way to the next street to the right of the main building, and to the rear of the building was a square building that was used for the laundry. It was a cement structure, on top of which was an area that we used to skate on, a big flat cement area.

Going out of the home through the front door and to the left of the building was a large area of grass, surrounded by a metal kind of fence. This seemed like a huge place to live. The matron said I could go out and play with the other kids. Well, I had my mind set on finding the boy who called me Spud. I found him sitting on a curb way out on the west side of the lawn area. The boy was collecting cigarette butts to make a whole cigarette to smoke. This boy was twelve or thirteen years of age, while I was just eight years old. He was tall and skinny, and I was short and quite stocky. Well, after he confirmed that he called me Spud, by calling me that again, I tore into him like a thunder storm of fists. The lessons my dad taught me on how to fight came in handy. I walked away satisfied that he would not call me that again. Later on, Lester and I became friends he really was a nice person. When I was out playing speedball with some of the boys, word of my encounter with Lester reached the other boys. As I walked away, several big boys came up to me and began calling me Spud. I took them on one at a time, but I just couldn't lick all of them. And besides being covered with dirt from head to toe, my nose was bleeding, and I sustained several bruises.

One of the male matrons came out to the fight and took me to Miss Wesley. About 30 minutes later, Miss Wesley came out and took me into her office.

She said that I have only been in the home for less than eight hours and look at the mess I was in, with dirt and blood from my nose and mouth on my clothes and face.

I thought she was going to whip me, but she wanted me to meld into the home as one of the boys. I told her what was said, and she said I should never let names become so harmful to my home life. "I don't know what to do with you, you are such a mess."

Miss Wesley called in Lester, who—I might add—was a bit dirty and bloody, and she made us apologize to each other and promise not to do this again. She let us out, and I soon found out that all the big boys were calling me Spud. And that is why defending myself got me a new name and a bloody nose. You know that they were getting bigger, and I couldn't fight them all, so the name Spud stuck until I left this home. Miss Holquist made me take a bath and go to bed without supper. For a boy that really enjoyed eating, that was a severe punishment indeed.

Our day started with a clean check by Miss Holquist and then onto breakfast. They fed us well at this home. After breakfast, we got to go out and play. I met a boy, John Braunly, and we had similar interests. John was a good skater, and we skated quite a bit on the old laundry room roof. We both could play marbles, and loved to play on the monkey bars. The field was used for softball games, which were always fun, along with speedball, that we played often. We played these games with the girls sometimes, but when the big boys played, the girls became scarce.

We did get to go to Central Grade School, a public school, and that pleased me to no end. My life at this home began to get better, and I became friends with some of the boys.

I chanced to run into the pantry just off the dining room in the basement area of the home. I looked over the cans, bottles and boxes, thinking I could find something to eat. I saw a bottle on the shelf that looked interesting, so I took it down to investigate. After opening the bottle, I smelled a smell that seemed good to me. I looked at the label on the bottle and it read Vinegar, so I proceeded to take a drink of the Vinegar. And it tasted quite good, so I drank some more and screwed the lid back on and left before someone caught me in the pantry. I continued to slip down and take a drink now and then when I could. After I left this home I never touched vinegar again. They had girls at the home, but I didn't remember much about them except that they liked roller skating and so did I, so I got to mix with everybody at the home.

The big boys tied up most of the time of the girls, who seemed a bit older than me. Sometimes the kids that had parents take them out for the weekends or Sundays, would invite me to go along. I can still remember when I was invited to go with the John Braunly's family for the weekend, and we went to an apartment building where they live. Along side of the building was a vacant lot, and we played baseball there. I can still remember the musty smell of the dirt we kicked up as we played.

I thought that was the best thing I got to do in the home. The kids' folks lived in a lower class area, according to John, but I didn't care about that. They served two great meals that day to me, and I thought that was quite nice. I just loved being a part of a family, even for a day. John's mother hugged John a lot and told him she loved him very much. I longed for that from my mom and dad. I thought that was a beautiful sight to see. John was a little embarrassed, it seemed. I longed for that from my mom, but that thought faded away pretty fast.

We went to these movies every Sunday morning. One thing about this home: they let the kids go to the church they wanted to or if the parents wanted them to attend. We got to see *Wolfman*, *The Mummy*, and even *Frankenstein*. The home would give us quarter, and we put it to good use—at the Upstage Theatre. We got to see a movie and get a bag of popcorn and a coke, for a quarter—how bad was that? I don't think the home ever got a complaint from the church since the kids could go to different Churches.

After seeing these movies, like *Frankenstein* and *Wolfman*, and, of course, *The Mummy*—in the Upstage Theater, I was terrified of these creatures and was sure they were going to get me sooner or later.

So many nights I saw the creature lurking outside of those windows. The curtains' moving shadows made it look like the creatures were here. I was so scared that on many nights, I was afraid to go to the bathroom for fear of being a victim to one of these creatures. Well, you guessed it. I ended up staying in bed and wetting my bed. I knew Miss Holquist would send me to Miss Wesley for punishment. That happened once and that's all. I couldn't stop being scared of the creatures, nor would I take a chance on getting caught with a wet bed.

We had several windows that faced to the north and they had fine Lennon curtains that moved at the slightest breeze. I was so hurt and ashamed when the matron spoke of my bed problem one morning in front of the other boys. So I put my thinking cap on and devised a plan. My plan was to get up when I knew I wet my bed and pull off the sheet that was wet. I opened the window right in front of my bed and hung the sheet out the window to dry.

To keep the sheet out there, I brought the window quietly down and closed it on the sheet edge. I stayed awake while the normal nightly breeze dried my sheet. I was sleeping on the edge of the mattress to let it dry out before I put the sheets on my bed and went to sleep as though nothing happened. I finally stopped wetting my bed, and stopped seeing creature movies. It seemed like one hand washed the other, and the end result was that I got up without fear and went to the bathroom.

One of the interesting things that seemed to go on in the home involved the field behind the home, which seemed to me to be quite big. A group of boys from a place called Lasco Creek, which was near the steel mills, came up to the back of the field behind the home.

They began by throwing rocks at us, and as soon as this happened, the big boys from the home went to work returning the favor to those boys. I learned later that the big boys had learned to make blackjacks, out of pieces of hose and stones, and slingshots. When the two sides began a fist fight, the blackjacks came out, and the boys used them on the Lasco Creek boys. It was amazing to me how accurate the sling shots were, and they did slow up the street gang of boys.

I know the matrons must have seen what was happening and tried to stop this fighting, but when they came out, the boys from Lasco Creek disappeared down the street.

The big boys at the home would not let me join them because I was too young.

One morning I was awakened early by Miss Holquist and told my mother was coming to pick me up and take me home. I was so excited, I got right out of bed and began to pack my clothes.

Miss Holquist said that she was coming early because she had to be at work later in the morning at a hospital in Colorado Springs. I know for sure that I came to the home January 1943. My mother never came to see me at the home. I watched for the cab to pull up right in front of the home's steps, and out stepped my mother.

# CHAPTER FIVE

---

## GROWING UP TOO FAST

What a beautiful sight. I was so happy I began to cry with joy. I hugged my mom so hard and for so long, I didn't want to let her go. I knew it was my mom because she wore the same perfume, and I loved the smell because it was of her. She told me she was taking me to live with her in Colorado Springs. I was so excited to see her.

It was interesting to note that years later I found out that my mother told the people at the homes that my father was deceased. She also told them that my father was a medical Doctor, a carpenter or a plumber, and that he died when I was quite young.

The father I knew was alive and well and he was so good to me. He lives in New Haven, Wyoming and I don't know any more about him. My mother meant well, I believe, but her priorities just didn't leave much room for her son.

My mother told the people at the McDermit Home for Children that I kept imagining things about my father and that I would try to contact him at the sheriff's office.

Needless to say that none of my letters ever went out. Later I found out that they had been destroyed by the homes. After I was taken out of the McDermit Home, I was to live with my mother in the Harlin Hotel in a city close by Colorado Springs. The town of Henderson was closer to her work. We lived in a small room in the hotel which was above the sporting goods store. Our first room window faced Theodore Street. Theodore Street was a busy street, and during the night, the neon lights on stores below and across the street at a dry goods store along with the streetlights would flash lights into our room. The traffic noise below on the street could get loud as well.

The hotel owner or manager finally moved us to a room down the hall on the left, which was much more peaceful for my mother's sleep. When I was alone in the room, which was every night until three or four in the morning, I had only a little radio to listen to in the room.

When my mother came home from her nursing job at three or four in the morning, she would kick me out of the room so she could sleep. Mom worked the same shift every day, from 3:00 p.m. to 11:00 p.m.

My mother had a bad temper and she got mad at me many, many times when I didn't want to go out into the street. This was especially true when it was cold or raining. She was a redheaded Irish lady and was very nice looking to the men that I had occasions to meet when they came by to see her. The hotel had a long stairway up from the street. I counted them once and found twenty-six stairs up, and then you would come down a long hallway to our room, which was on the left side of the hallway.

Our room had a small window, which showed a wall on the building next door. Since it was much safer for me to go out when mother came home than to stay and get a beating from her short temper, I left for Theodore and Newland streets soon after her arrival at our hotel room. Once when I was headed out, I passed a man walking up the stairs and down the hall towards our room. He walked right into our room without knocking.

Fearing for my mother's safety, I ran back toward the room calling out to Mom. When I got to the door she was at the door fearing something had happened to me. She said the man was a friend dropping by to say hello. This was about four thirty in the morning. I began waiting around for a week or so, and Mom had a lot of friends.

I began to go up and down the street and into my favorite store, Patrillos, which had parched corn, as they called it. I loved the parched corn and every time I had a little money, I got myself some.

Next door was a fine Chinese Restaurant, and every morning, the owner came out to stand along the walk just after he came to work. I began to go up and down the street. In general, people were very nice to me, and I liked that, because it meant to me that I must be ok! Otherwise they wouldn't be so nice to a stranger. I became friendly with him, and one day, noticing that I was a bit sleepy, he suggested that I come into the back booth and lie down for awhile.

Well every day after that, I would come down to the restaurant and get some sleep. He was curious as to why I was downtown so early every day. I told him the story of my mother's temper and that I was better off out of the hotel room. He fed me a few times.

During the day, I would roam the streets looking for something to do. I ran into a man that delivered papers to the new facility at Fort Carson, the military base south of town. He let me go with another boy, Allan, to sell papers at the mess hall at the fort. The mess hall was the first building to be built to feed the workers on the fort property. The boy was about thirteen and he was glad to have company selling the papers. Allan was a nice guy and we had a lot of laughs working the mess hall.

Allan was a colored boy, and he certainly had some selling tricks up his sleeve. We would tell the GI workers that if we could guess their state of birth, then they would pay double; if not the paper was free. Allan used states like the state of ignorance, and state of infancy. It was fun but the MPs picked us up and sent us back to town with a warning not to come on the base again. That was the end of my very short career selling newspapers.

On one of my daily journeys, I watched some shoeshine boys at a shoe repair shop. These boys, mostly colored, could make music when they shined shoes. I was amazed at the speed that these boys would go to shine the shoes. I asked one of the boys how they learned to do this kind of work. They introduced me to Tom, and he talked to me about why I was out on the street. Tom asked me if I had eaten today and of course, I had not. He took me into a sandwich shop close by on Theodore Street and bought me lunch.

He offered me a job on the shine line. there was one stand still open. Needless to say, I learned to make the shine rag sing. We put polish on shoes, rag shine the polish, then we sprinkled the shoe with water and shined the shoe to a glisten. We got a nickel a shine, and let me tell you I felt rich with money in my pocket.

I didn't keep all the money I earned. The customers, mostly men, would pay Mr. Tom twenty-five cents.

The boys that had been there for sometime had developed a talent for tossing their coins closest to the wall outside of the store and would collect all the coins of the losers, of which this novice was one. This was the reason my funds went down. However, I did get something to eat during the day. Tom was a colored man and was a fine human being and cared very much for his customers and workers alike. I learned a lot about human love from Tom. He was so good to his boys on the shine line.

The shine boys, as we were called, also showed me how to toss coins to a line in the sidewalk. This was their way of gambling. One of the boys, Johnson, told me about a night job he had at Fast Lanes on Nevada Street, in Colorado Springs. I went with him to the bowling alley on Nevada and got a job setting pins for bowlers.

We were given a nickel a line. Plus if we were fast picking up the pins and setting the rack down for the next bowler, we sometimes would get a tip thrown down the alley. My biggest tip was a fifty-cent piece. Each pinsetter would be responsible for two alleys. We sat on a partition between the alleys, and after they bowled, we would jump into the pin area, collect the pins, put them in the rack as fast as we could, and then pull the rack down to the floor and release the racks holding the pins. There was some danger in setting the pins because the pins would fly out of the floor into the collection area and hit the boy pinsetter. Luckily I was never hit and again got some change in my pocket.

Most of my change went for food and a daily run to Patrillos for some of her great parched corn.

My mother never questioned me about what I was doing. You see, I went home before she had to leave for work at 10;00 or 11:00 p.m. as a nurse. I told her I met some other boys and went to play ball with them during the day.

The Chinese man at the restaurant finally told me I couldn't sleep in the back booth any more. However, I made a mistake and did one more time. The sheriff came by and threw me out of the restaurant.

While I was setting pins at the bowling alley, one of the bowlers, a gentleman, came back to the pin-setting area to talk to me. I was afraid he was going to say I was too slow in my pin-setting work. He gave me seventy-five cents and said I was the best setter he has had the privilege of using.

He also said the company he worked for needed a boy who was willing to work hard for a special job. He told me I had to have a social security card. I could get one by going into the Social Security Office in Colorado Springs. Boy, was I a happy camper. I got the card at nine years old and felt like an adult. I did not tell my mother for fear she would not let me work.

The new job was at the Aloha Film Company just north of town on Nevada Street which became a highway going out of town. The building I was to work at was huge, and I was a little leery of going into the building. I went in and talked with a lady at the front desk who directed me to the man that I came into contact with at the bowling alley. Mr. Wilson introduced me to a man who handled the maintenance for the company's property. George was his name, and he sat me down and made me feel a lot better about the job.

My only job was to pick out the dandelions from the massive front lawn in front of the building. I showed George my Social Security card I received at 9 years of age, and he filled out some papers on me so I would get paid.

I did well for the first three weeks, and on the fourth week, I fell asleep on the lawn. George awakened me and got me going again, with a warning that the company could not tolerate sleeping on the job. The next week I did a good job, but again on Wednesday, I fell asleep on the lawn. Well, that cooked my goose, and George had to fire me. I really felt important on that job. I had tears in my eyes, and George tried to console me. However, it hurt me to be fired. I left the McDermit Home in the fall, and leaves were on the ground. I think it was late fall 1944. I thought about that home and wondered how my friends were at the home. The one thing about the home is I always had a warm bed and three meals a day.

I missed my father in Wyoming very much. He was like a big light in my life that kept me secure and happy in my memories of New Haven, Wyoming. I wrote letters to my dad to New Haven, Wyoming, but never heard from him since we left. I had a difficult time with this, and Mother told me he had died.

Here I am still setting pins and shining shoes at shoe repair shop. At least I didn't get fired from these jobs.

One day the police came by and was questioning me about who I was and where I lived. I wouldn't tell them anything, so they hauled me off to the police department. I was being questioned so much, but I knew I couldn't give them my name or my mother's name or where I lived. They said there was no missing boy's report, so they kept questioning me.

Finally, they took me into the chief of police's office. His name was Dad Billings, and he looked like a bulldog sitting behind the desk. Dad Billings did not say anything for two or three minutes, and then he pounded on his desk and said I better tell him what he wants to know. He scared me so much I started peeing in my pants. I told him that I could not tell him because my mother would beat me.

He finally convinced me that the officers would take me back to the hotel. I knew my mother in spite of his statement that they would be sure she wouldn't do just that. As we approached the hotel I told the officers that there is a long stairway up to the first floor, and then a long walk back to the room on the left.

My mother answered the door and the officers told her not to beat me or punish me in any way. She acted like she had been looking for me for three days and was so happy that I was returned to her. She promised not to punish me, and believe me I knew that was a lie. I hated to see the officers go, and my mother and I watched them as they went down the hall and headed down the stairs.

As soon as they were out of sight my mother began trying to beat me with anything she could pick up, including the lamp on the nightstand. I did what I usually had to do. I ran around the room until I reached the door and ran out and down the hall. The landlady heard the commotion, and called the police who came right away. They took me down to the welfare people who decided I should go to a foster home.

They put me into a foster home with people who were very religious. They wore long dresses mostly black, with a black small beanie-like cap on top of their heads. They had three goats on the property down close to the creek bed. I had never tasted goat milk before, and I wasn't sure I wanted to now. Goat's milk is sweet, and they poured it through a cloth to filter it. They convinced me it was fine, and I need to drink milk for my health. I was enrolled into a grade school on the west side of an area called Potter City.

I made some friends at school and seemed to get along with the teachers and kids in the school. My freckles and red hair gave me a few problems, but I managed to get through them without too much fighting.

Two of the kids always walked home with me before they went to their home. The family attended church two or three times a week. On Sunday, we went to one of the buildings down in town and went to the second floor. This was a huge room with benches going down both sides of the room and down the center.

They sang songs and I liked that, but I didn't like kneeling on the floor while several men prayed and recited the Bible. They all had on the black clothes on with beanies like the folks with which I lived. I met a little girl that went to our school at this church, and we sat next to one another. They were friends of the family I was living with named Jordon. The Jordon family was really involved in the ceremonies going on. Cindy, the girl from school that was sitting next to me, was a lot of fun.

She acted like some of the people who stood up and shouted sayings that I had never heard before. When they all got on their knees to pray Cindy and I stayed on our bench. We had some fun pointing at different looks of people across this big room. The next time we went to the church, we were not allowed to sit together, but we did signal hello from where we sat. We stayed in our seats, however, and were good kids. One afternoon, I rode one of the goats down the creek a short distance, and it was fun.

The next three days when my friends and I came home from school we rode the goats down on the creek bed and back, my buddies had a great time with the goats. We rode the goats every afternoon after that first time. I was surprised that no one came down there when we were riding.

Mr. Jordon called me into his Bible study room to talk to me. He said the goats were not delivering the milk they should, and his investigation told him why.

Well, needless to say, I had to bend over and get the belt in the name of the Lord. I often wondered if the Lord knew about all of these welts that were credited to him. In less than one week, the welfare people came to pick me up and move me to another foster home. The new foster home was a religious home similar to the other home.

The folks here were clad in long gowns and black beanies just as were the first foster home. One of the brethren told me it was a Mennonite church. I like the music and could sing along with the group of singers.

I didn't make it here in this foster home, and it wasn't long before the welfare people came to pick me up and send me to the Lord's Home for Children.

# CHAPTER SIX

## THE LORD'S HOME FOR CHILDREN

The Lords Home for Children was a far different place than the Foster Homes. It was more in the line of the McDermit Home in looks when we drove through the gates and up into the driveway that went in front of the home. We got out of the car and went inside of the big three or four-storied building. We were taken back to the rear of the building to meet a tall man with glasses called Daddy Joseph, and his wife called Mother Louise.

Something didn't set right with me when I heard the names they were to be called. I thought of my mother and my father and knew they were the only parents I had somewhere. I could not, and would not, call them anything but uncle and aunt. After all, I had none of those.

The welfare workers talked with me and told me I would really like living in this home. They also advised me that my mother had been told that I would be coming here to this home and should come to see me whenever she so desired.

I never heard from my mother or father for several years—in fact, never from my father. Daddy Joseph asked a Miss Swans to take me on a tour of the premises.

She said she was the home secretary, and if I had any questions that I should feel free to come to her office and come right in to talk with her. The routine seemed the same as it did at the McDermit Home. I was taken on a tour of the place and the grounds. I was introduced to several adults as a new boy that has come to stay with us. All the matrons were called uncle or aunt and the director of the home, Daddy Joseph and his wife, Mother Louise, ran the home. Daddy Joseph was a preacher as well, and if the truth were known, this was his real calling and where his heart seemed to be at. This impression I felt and believed after being in the home a couple of years.

All the boys lived on the third floor of the home. The home was ordered by the City of Colorado Springs to build a fire escape. This put a small deck outside of our entry to the fire escape window.

This gave us access to the roof. We never fell or slid down the roof while going up or down. We would steal cans of Spam from the kitchen, bring them up here, take them up to the top of the roof, and enjoy a feast of Spam we had retrieved. Later in my twenties, I looked at the roof, and it scared me to think we went up that grade without falling down. It seems kids don't fear a lot of experiences and the risks involved.

We used to throw the empty cans off of the roof as far as we could get them, which, was about seventy feet away from the house, on to a grassy area and retrieve them early in the morning before the matrons could see them. Later, when the home was stockpiling walls for the new boys' dorm, we then threw with talent to land them on the big stacks of lumber. Then the first thing in the morning, we would go out and clean them up and put them in the home's trash bin.

We continued to do this even after they put a big stack of lumber next to the driveway and in line with the usual spot where we threw the cans. We got a lot more distance out of the cans by flattening them first. The lumber was given to the home from a construction company that was tearing down old barrack buildings.

The home was going to use the lumber to build a brand new boys dorm that would house the big and little boys. Well, that will do it in for our deck tossing when it was finally built. The day we explored the third floor, we went back into the roomy space outside the attic wall of the big room itself. Low and behold we found a complete skeleton hanging from the ceiling in this attic area. We named it from the name Murphy scribbled on the wall next to the skeleton, so we called it Murphy. I

There were about six big boys that stayed in the room on third floor. The oldest boy got the front room with a deck which looked out over the front driveway and to the front gate. It was a great room, and we were jealous of the older boys who were thirteen and twelve years old.

Daddy Joseph never knew about our little dining room that we set up back in the attic under the eaves area beyond our guest, Murphy. We were able to keep this little area where we stored our cans of fruit and Spam that the home generously provided for us.

I failed to mention the kitchen was at the bottom of the maid's stairway on the first floor. We were all assigned jobs in the kitchen and elsewhere around the home. It gave us the perfect opportunity to know the kitchen and pantries well. We were the kings of the home since we did have a secret bartering position from third floor.

The home was also a home to the Haslet family. Jim Haslet and Grandpa Clemont took care of the maintenance. He and Jim rarely came up to third floor. As I have grown older, I can understand their reluctance to visit our floor—there were no elevators or lifts.

Jim and Grandpa never knew about our little dining room either. We kept this a secret for some time until; we moved out of the building, which I believe was at the end of my second year at the home.

Mrs. Haslet ran the kitchen. She cooked good food.

Since we were all assigned jobs in the kitchen and elsewhere around the home, there seemed to be no shortage of jobs at the home.

Our matron was called Delila, and she was an ex-first sergeant in the British Army. It didn't take me long to know who was the boss when she was around. She still thought she was in the army and ran the place that way.

One thing you didn't want to do was to get her mad. I often thought how she acted very much like my mother when she became angry. Del, as we called her, was a lot different than Mom. She was able to talk to us, and it didn't take long for us to use this interest to our benefit

On one occasion when she took Junior Peloni and me up to the third floor to receive our whippings we asked her what it was like in the army. Well, needless to say, we listened to her story, and when she was through telling us the tale, she said, "You boys run along and try to be good and do the right thing". We never forgot that experience, and we used it many times.

I wish when I was with my mother, that she would have enjoyed telling me some stories. My mother would not let me talk about my dad or anything about New Haven, Wyoming. I never heard from my father or my mother for years after arriving in this home.

Delila used switches that we got to pick out of the growth of many bushes in the front by the driveway. She would allow us to pick out the switches based on how old we were at that time. We learned the hard way the thick switches would hurt more but would break quicker than the thin switches.

The thin switches would sting a lot but would last a whole lot longer. The five year olds could pick out five switches; and the thirteen-year-olds, thirteen switches In the front of the home, there was a little grove of big bushes which were the source of our selection of switches.

I think the theory behind this selection was that the older boys, who were getting more switches due to the age, would choose to not do anything that would put them in harm's way. As to switching, Del was fair in her punishments, and that was a mark in her favor. There were times when the men matrons or Daddy Joseph would give us a whipping.

The area on which the whippings would land was between the neck and the ankles. When one of the men whipped you, they believed they were doing it in God's name, so they wanted to be complete in that effort. They always said it hurt them worse than it did us—how did they know? They assumed we were not too bright, I suspect. I wondered if God even knew of the punishments.

The home was a good place because we had a large playground to do all kinds of things recreational. Some of the games we played were kick the can, softball, a merry-go-round marbles, kickball and basketball out on the barn where the basket was put.

I liked kick the can because the girl I liked always played that, and sometimes we got to hide behind a bush next to the south gate. We never did anything out of line, but just being together away from the other kids was a satisfying exercise. I liked the softball games because we played them at school, and they were great games.

I think the home softball games helped me become a good ball player at school.

Miss Balt, my sixth-grade teacher and the gym teacher, was the most encouraging teacher to boost me along in sports. I became one of the outstanding grade school players when playing Colorado Springs schools. I was very efficient at the plate in batting. Then we had these city track meets. Now let me tell you, I was not a good runner although I tried very hard to be. My area was the shot put and the broad jump.

We moved into the new dorm and our new Matron, Richard Woolsey, at the time was from New Jersey. Dick, as he was called, was an ex-professional wrestler.

It did not take long for us to find out about his type of discipline. He used his fist and powerful arms to give us our beatings. Let me tell you, his punishment was brutal. Richard Woolsey, as are all the matrons who worked in the home, was called to take care of children by the Lord. When the welts opened the matron just put iodine or Merthiolate on the wounds, and it did sting. Most of the time they just left welts on the back and legs.

I often wondered why my buttocks, even though it was hit, didn't show any welts, too much fat, I guess. He believed in the type of discipline that incorporated the use of fists. He had big strong arms, and when he hit you, it sent you across the room in a slide at times, but always with a painful spot where he was able to hit.

He believed that the area from the neck down was fair game for hitting. His arms looked like tree trunks hanging from his shoulders.

Believe me, the switches of Del, or the belts of Daddy Joseph were far less welt designing on your body. His daughter Dorine was in my class, and let me tell you, all of my sins of lateness in my home room now became common knowledge to the Woolsey family, and especially Dick. That bit of knowledge brought about a whipping by Dicks' fists and left me in pain.

I told Miss Broem that the situation had developed, and I would make a concerted effort to get to class on time from now on. She did question me about my bruises on the arms and shoulders, knowing that Mr. Woolsey's daughter was in my class. I didn't tell her where they came from. Instead I told her it was from sports.

Dorine praised herself on being a snitch for her. South Junior opened a new day for me in sports through gym classes right after school. You see, the home's bus took us to school and picked us up at noon and after school. We went home for lunch and had Bible verse contests at the lunch tables. At breakfast, we read *Pilgrim's Progress* or some other godly book.

We carried bruises for some time. He particularly liked the back and arms as targets of his fierce attempts to keep us in line. We had no angels in the boys' dorm, and certainly, I was not one of the prized boys in the home.

When Mr. Woolsey and his family got ready to journey back to New Jersey, we noticed that he was loading all kinds of toys from the little boys' dorm and from our gym in the basement. We went to Daddy Joseph and told him what we had seen. After all, we didn't like him at all and were so glad to see him go.

Life with Dick Woolsey was a terrible life and finally, for some reason, the Woolsey's were asked to leave the home. I really believe the Lord had enough of their care for us. We watched him load his rented truck for the journey back to Pennsylvania. We watched him load up all of the toys from little boy's dorm up into the truck. He was ready to go.

Another boy, named Junior Peloni and I went to Daddy Joseph and told him that the Woolsey's had taken almost all of the little boys toys. Daddy Joseph went out to his truck to check before he drove off and asked to look inside of his rental truck to see if he had taken any of boys' toys, as the boys stated.

When he finally agreed to open up the back, low and behold, there in the truck were all of the toys that were donated to the Lord's Home. Daddy Joseph made him remove the toys that belonged to the boys. Not a word was spoken by either man after it was emptied of all of the toys for the little boys.

Daddy Joseph impressed me as being a strong man with courage and in the name of God. Over the next few years, I was able to have discussions with Daddy Joseph.

He wore his watch on the inside of his left wrist. I asked him about this because everyone else wore their watches on the outside of their wrists.

He told me that when he did any work or reading that he could see the inside of his wrist much easier than turning it over so he could see the time. Well, needless to say, when I became older and could wear a watch, I wore it on the inside of my left wrist, for many years, he made sense.

Sometimes when we would play other schools in baseball, I often wondered what it would be like had my mother left me with my stepfather in New Haven, Wyoming. The kids we met at these games were great to me, especially Joe Booker, a player from Helen Hurst School.

Joe was their best player, and in the games we played them, he and I competed. And as a result, we became great friends that lasted into high school. Joe was a terrific athlete. Joe had some skills that I didn't have. He could high jump very high and won most city meets in that event. I broad jumped and seemed to always get second or third place—cost of being a bit chubby.

We had some fine people at the home from time to time. Just to mention a few, Artie Bells was very impressive as a woman. She was about forty and was from Arkansas. She could swing an axe better and longer than any of the big boys could. She never had a harsh word for any of us when we petered out on the job or were just lazy.

She talked to the boys about the work side of life and helped make us realize that we would someday have to make the decision to earn a living by working. She was a fine and Godly woman.

Aunts Clorine and Hilda were the nurses in the infirmary. This building was originally for the servants and guests that either worked at the ranch or were visitors, as would commonly happen.

I was put in the infirmary once when the measles were going through the home. I believe I was eleven at the time. They explained to me that since I didn't get the disease, they quarantined me. All the kids got the disease, so I was sent to school from the infirmary and back in an old suburban. Later in life, at the ripe old age of twelve, I came down with appendicitis.

Again, I was the guest of the infirmary until I recovered. I was in the hospital for about three weeks. I left the hospital with a four-inch scar.

I met Leona in the hospital and saw her come by my room every day I was there. I would have been out sooner, but I was racing this girl in a wheelchair. She was also twelve and was in there for some other reason. There was a tunnel from one building to another at St. Florence Hospital, and it was about 150 yards long by my guess. Leona and I would go around the hospital and say hi to the other patients.

One morning, we got the idea we could have a race down that tunnel because there was not much traffic early in the morning at about six o'clock. Little did I know that Leona knew the tunnel much better than I. So off we went down the tunnel. It went downhill a bit from the outer building to the main building. We were doing fine until I failed to make the turn at the end of the tunnel and smashed into the wall.

Leona made it, wouldn't you know, and was laughing as we both sat there in the hall. Well, I tore open the incision on my appendix operation. That made me stay for a week longer and I was ordered to stay in my room, which I was glad to do. Leona came to see me until she had to leave and go home. I often wondered whatever happened to Leona. I really enjoyed the breakfast, lunch, and dinner in bed. They served me great food, and the nurses would cheat a little and give me some extra food. When I went back to the Lord's Home I had to stay in the infirmary for a week under observation. My appendix operation left a scar about four-inches long still in spite of the fall in the tunnel.

During the later part of my second year of life at the home, we got new matrons: Todd and Janet Wilts. He was a tall Scotsman, and she was all Irish, temper and all.

Boy, we were fortunate to have them as matrons. They were the closest matrons to a family. Uncle Todd came closest to making a family out of the boys that he supervised. I will talk more about them later.

Before Uncle Todd and Aunt Janet came to the home, we had several other folks that had an impact on our lives. Ken Berry, an older man from Boulder, came down to help Daddy Joseph run things here at the home. Daddy Joseph was first a preacher of the Bible and traveled around the country given lectures at the assemblies. This was a nondenominational group of Christians gathered all around the country.

I once ask Daddy Joseph why they call it nondenominational when it separates itself as a special group, just like the Catholics.

His answer was not complete for me. He said they are committed to the Word of God as it is written and have no known denominational title, such as do Catholics and Methodists. I later found out that in California they are called Plymouth Brethren because in California they had to have a name.

To this day, I do not think his answer was complete enough to satisfy an inquiring mind bound up in the daily Christian philosophy that we ate, drank, and slept on every day.

I had a lot of respect for Daddy Joseph. He was harsh at times, but at other times, he spoke with you as though you might have a brain that could understand some of his thinking. I was constantly challenged by not what he said but how he said it.

As I mentioned earlier, we had some sort of Christian training every day and it seemed that it was all day; however, it was not. I loved the music that we sang and I did sing every song.

After the evening service, we went out to play whatever we could get going. We would play some softball with definite limitations. We did not have enough room to smack the ball out of the area for some serious scoring. My happiest moments were when we were released after the evening meeting of preaching, prayer and singing to go out to play.

The fences were too close for the big boys. As we grew older and bigger, we tended to hit the ball out of the grounds of the home.

Nobody at the home knew my name was Spud, and I never told them, until a family of ours came up from the McDermit Home in Pueblo who knew me as Spud and also knew that I hated to be called Spud. Well, needless to say, it stuck, and I soon was called by the name of Spud from all the matrons and other adult helpers. The family was the Stard family, Weseter (a big guy and the oldest), then came Curley, Nadine, and finally Geneen. It took me a long time to forgive them for bringing the name with them from the McClelland Home. Perhaps that is what the Lord wanted; however, I doubt that as well. He never asked me for my input.

The right time came around when we had to tell Daddy Joseph about the skeleton we found in the attic area.

He scolded us but no spanking came from him this time. Daddy Joseph knew nothing about the skeleton. However, he couldn't let a chance for a sermon pass him by.

All kinds of stories went traveling around about the skeleton, and finally, Daddy Joseph got rid of the skeleton. He forbade us from talking to anyone about the skeleton, and no one seemed to know about it, including the previous owners who had no idea it was hung on a little chain, attached to the beam coming down from the attic sealing. We boys became heroes in our own minds.

I often wondered who that skeleton represented in full body form and where did it come from. I asked Daddy Joseph many times over the course of my life and got the same answer, "We don't know and we don't care, it was before our time at the ranch."

I was thirteen, and it was about this time in my life that Uncle Todd told me my mother was coming to pick me up and take me on a vacation to Wyoming. Well, you can imagine my excitement, and when tears came running down my cheeks, Uncle Todd put his arm around me and said, "Son, you have a great time with your mother."

My mother came up in a taxi and I was at the front gate to meet her. I could hardly see her for I was crying with joy so much. I gave her a hug, and when I pressed against her side and felt her arms around me, I could smell her perfume and knew it was my mom.

The taxi took us up to the bus station just across from the post office, a familiar area to me. We went inside, and Mom bought fares to the north end of town. We got out and walked about 2 blocks to the highway, and Mom began thumbing a ride to Denver. I guess she had no money.

A trucker picked us up, and we three sat in the cab. The driver, Jim, was a nice man who lived in Colorado Springs. Mom told him she had run out of money but needed to get us to Cheyenne, Wyoming. The cab of the truck had a terrible odor. The man chewed tobacco, and he had a gallon can down below my feet on the floor. The gallon can was like that of the cans of tomatoes and other vegetables that came into the kitchen for food. The man would spit to the can and hit it. He put a big cloth over Mom's lap, and I held the can up so it wouldn't splash on me. Although, to the man's credit, he never missed hitting the can, and no splash.

The nice man said he would give Mom the money to buy bus fare from Denver to Cheyenne. He was going to Denver and would drop us at the bus depot. Mom said she would send him back his money as soon as she went to work in Colorado Springs.

The bus depot was busy with a lot of people and Mom made sure I stuck close to her. Mom took me over to stand by the ladies room because of the big crowd of people in the bus station. Mom hit the food machines so we could have something to eat. Once on the bus it didn't take me long to fall asleep.

We finally arrived at Cheyenne. Mom's boyfriend, Gus Russell, met us and took us to a hotel in Cheyenne. The hotel was called the Rio Hotel and this is where Gus worked as a day clerk.

Mom and I stayed in room 216, and across the hall was Gus's room, number 213. Mom and I were very tired, and we went to bed right away. I didn't bring any pajamas, and Mom said it was fine or I could sleep in my shorts. It wasn't long and we fell asleep.

The next morning, we went out for a great breakfast at the corner café just down the street from the hotel. After breakfast, Gus took me on a tour of the city. He showed us the area where the famous rodeo, the Frontier Days, happened. When we got back to the hotel, Gus said there was a theatre just around the corner where they showed current movies. I took in the movies every day. The theater showed two or three movies a day, and then another at 6:00 p.m.

One night on our fourth day there, the movies let out early, and I went to the hotel to see Mom and go to bed. I went in to the hotel and up to our room. Mom wasn't there, so I went to Gus's room. Mom and Gus were naked, having sex and I surprised them—and myself. Mom sat up in bed and told me to go to our room and crawl into bed. She would be along soon.

I went to bed and was soon asleep. Mom woke me up when she got into bed later. Mom began rubbing her hands over my body and kept saying, "Will you love me tomorrow?" I kept saying "I would love you forever, Mom." This went on for a few minutes, and finally, she got a hold of my penis and began playing with it. Mom moved me on top of her, and inserted me into her. Pretty soon after, we were both going up and down. I heard Mom let out a loud noise, and just about the same time, I felt a great rush in my body that felt so very good. I loved my Mom and thought, *What a great experience with my mom.* It felt so good, and it was my mom who gave me that wonderful feeling. Mom didn't say another word as she rolled over, and we went sleep.

The next morning when I awoke, I began moving my hand over her beautiful body, especially her breasts, which were quite large.

When I found her red hair between her legs, Mom grabbed my hand and told me to get up and to quit doing what I was doing. She seemed mad when she told me to get dressed so we could go to breakfast. We woke Gus up, and the three of us went off to breakfast. Mom did not say one word, and I thought that I did something wrong to make her angry. Mom finally said that I would be going home today on the bus. She said this wasn't working out and told Gus that she wanted him to take me to the bus depot after breakfast. Gus took me up to the room to get my things. I asked him why mom was so mad at me. He said that Mom gets mad at different times, and he doesn't know why.

I got on the bus, and Mom was still angry and didn't even say good-bye or "I love you, Bobby." I began to cry. As the bus pulled away, tears began to soak my shirt, and I could no longer see through the tears. And she faded from sight.

Daddy Joseph once told me that he believed that I was responsible for much of the wrong deeds that showed up at the home. He said I was like a cat. They knew I was behind everything, but they could not find my tracks—very much like a cat. I told him over and over that I was not responsible, but he somehow kept attaching the blame to me but could not justify it enough to punish me for what happened.

There were times when I knew I had nothing to do with the wrongness, but I may have known who was responsible; however, I just would not tell the matrons or Daddy Joseph.

## FINDING SPORTS

As I mentioned earlier, we had some sort of Christian training every day, and it seemed that it was all day. However, it was not too long and we went out to play ball. During this period of time we were getting more Christian helpers, and the new dorm was being built, between the north gate and the main building.

We had several adult men who at times were matrons or assistants to Daddy Joseph. The home was a good place because we had a large playground to do all kinds of things recreational. We never did anything out of line, but just being together away from the other kids was a satisfying exercise.

The kids we met at the softball games were great to me, especially Joe Booker, a player from Helenic Grade School. Joe was their best player and in the games we played against them, he and I competed, and as a result we became great friends that lasted into High School.

Joe was a terrific athlete, and when we arrived at the Junior High we teamed up to take all comers. Joe was an all-around exceptional athlete. In basketball, we were hard to beat and both chosen to play for the high school junior varsity team. Joe was a colored boy who had more talent in his little finger than most have in their whole body. In junior high, we always covered each other in sports and chose to be on the same team. I remember when Joe and I got our warm-up uniforms and played on the high school team. Even though we were in ninth grade at the junior high school, we got to play with the high school team—a real compliment to our ability. We both lettered in our freshman year in junior high with a high school letter.

At that time, you don't think of it that way, but we were just thrilled to death that we were allowed to play. John Morris was the JV coach at the high school. He was also the winning coach of the football team which went sixteen seasons and never had a losing season. He was something else. I kept track of Joe Booker for a long time and finally lost track of him when I grew older and left the home.

In junior high school, it seemed a lot of fights went on for no reason. The school was 60 percent minority students from this area. This may have been a reason for these fights.

I remember the boys from Park Valley, a mining community about twenty miles north of town. These boys were mostly Latinos, and their families must have had a hard time economically. These boys were fine athletes and excelled in every sport. It was interesting for me to find out that the school district didn't want them to go to the junior high in the north part of the city, which was much closer for them to be bused. This was an upper-class neighborhood, and it seemed that the busing to the junior high in the south part of town reflected that sentiment.

At South Junior, my home room teacher, Miss Broem, was a little old lady that was so good to me. We had homeroom meetings every morning for fifteen minutes.

We boys were out on the playground having a speedball game. This game was like soccer except you could pass the ball with your hands if it was kicked up to you by another player. You could run with the ball and pass it until you got to the goal and then you could kick it through. It was a different game than today's popular game of soccer. The game was called speedball.

There were times when we got so involved in our pre-school game of speedball that we went past the tardy bell for homerooms.

We ran like heck into the building. Some of the kids didn't have Miss Broem, and as a result, they usually got into trouble with the principal's office. Miss Broem would put her arm around me and ask me if we won of lost. Then she would have me run down to the bathroom and wash my hands and face from the dust we kicked up on the playing field. She was always there for me, and in turn, I tried very hard to get good grades in her geography class. I loved that little old lady; she made me feel worth something. Later as a teacher, I went up to see her in her home in the Broadmoor area several times until she passed away.

The Dorley family of five kids, one girl, and four boys, came to live with us at the Lord's Home for Children. Elrod and Thona both had red hair—as you can see, I had redheaded company for playmates. Thona was older than all of the boys. She was nice person and seemed to always include me in her family thinking. The two younger boys, Frank and Kyle, made up the contingency of the Dorley family in the home. Walrod was a runner who held up the running end of athletes at the home. He just seemed to run like a deer and didn't seem to wind like this redhead writing this story. You see, I was shorter and a chubby boy, so running was not my deal. After I left the home, they went to live with their mother in California.

Later in life, I saw their mother, who lived in Hayward, and she brought me up to date on the family. Frank was dying of cancer in a Reno hospital—that left an empty space in my heart, a space that became filled with sadness. The children from the home were really the only family I had at that time. I wanted to talk to Frank who apparently knew my son Richard who lived in San Francisco, but he was dying in a hospital in Reno, Nevada. I wanted to talk to him but it was too late.

A family of two came to live at the home, Anower and Annie Marie Freaney. Anower was a year younger than I, and Annie Marie was a year older than I. Annie Marie was a beautiful girl, and she was always a lady when we all went out to play. The two of them left after about two years and returned to Pennsylvania.

The Wilson family of five came to live in the home. Jerome was one year older than I, Margo, Bertha, and Jason were closer to my age, up or down. a few months. Jason was a good athlete, Jerome was always willing to play games with the rest of the kids, but I sensed his heart was not in the activity. Bertha was my age, and she sure had her share of boys in high school. I think Jerome left the home at eighteen, and I lost track of the Wilson family when they left to live with their mother up in Denver. When this family came up from the McDermit Home, they brought with them my known name of Spud.

I never told anybody at the Lord's Home that my name was Spud until the Wilson family landed at the Lord's Home for Children in Colorado Spring. This family came up from the McDermit Home

Well as you have guessed I had a rough time for a while. Many scrapes and dirty, bloody faces—mine as well as their faces—were dirty from rolling in the dirt. Jerome Wilson usually had his way in these local gatherings. After all, he was taller and much bigger than we were. But I would offer that on many occasions, there was a bigger fight in the smaller boys than the fight in the bigger boys. In any case, Jerome and the other boys all became friends.

When you are restricted to staying in one place during the free time available, the grounds of the home become very small indeed. Since I was junior in size and age to this big fellow Jerome, I had to live with the transfer of my nickname of Spud. It became the source of scuffles at school as well. I reached junior high school, a school that was dominated by the majority of the minority population. Now, if you will, transfer the fact that I was a fiery redhead with a multitude of freckles, then you will get the picture of my rowdy behavior at the junior high level.

Daddy Joseph always told us the sports activities outside of the home grounds were for kids off of the streets. Let me tell you, many times I was disciplined for disagreeing with Daddy Joseph and other matrons. The home stood on approximately three acres of ground, so you see, we didn't have all that much play area.

The home kept me from joining teams so I could learn sports from those who had been playing all there known lives. The very idea of identifying kids off the street differently from us was absurd.

After all, we were all kids of the streets, and as such, we needed to rub shoulders, at least in sports, with those of-the-street kids that we went to school and sat through classes with us until the bell changed the musical rooms game. To this day, I believe that Jesus, who stood for all sinners and any others, did not discriminate, as did the home operatives at the Lord's Home for Children. Daddy Joseph always maintained that the kids of the streets were not like us, and as a result, he told us the school sports were for them, not for us. If it were not for Uncle Todd letting me sneak uptown to the Boys Club, to play with the kids of the streets, I would not have played for the high school team in basketball.

The home did teach us to have principles to live by, and this was particularly true of Uncle Todd and Aunt Janet.

I was baptized and accepted Jesus as my savior on April 15, 1949.

Todd and Janet were good to me after I came back to the home at fifteen years old. They were more responsible for making the boys' dorm a family affair. Uncle Todd understood the needs and benefits of sports in our lives. He encouraged us in that direction, even though it was counter to the home's policies.

They were devout Christians but with a conviction of what it meant to bring Christianity and the real world to a better understanding of just what a family should be.

Many of the people, who have been in experiences with me, both personal and in sports and business, have always commented on the patience that I possessed.

This I attribute to Uncle Todd entirely. Aunt Janet was an Irish lady who had short fuses that Todd had to extinguish often before it ended up on us boys.

Daddy Joseph was more of a scholar, and often, since my home days, I thought his calling would be in a Christian college. I credit my inquisitive fertile mind with the many conversations with this man. He allowed me to reach out with questions that required answers that took into effect philosophical discussions which sought to bring together the Bible teachings with the life around me.

Daddy Joseph was like an intellectual conduit through which flowed challenges to the various premises from both the secular and spiritual world. This was the secular and spiritual worlds that I could understand in my early teen years.

Since I had no real affiliation with a father and a mother during these years, the name stuck with me. I began to believe Spud was my real name that my mother must have uttered to the McDermit Home director, Miss Dudley.

## LONELINESS

For so many years I wanted to talk with someone about my relationship with my mother. I kept burying it deeper inside of me, knowing that it was wrong, and I didn't want to be whipped or disciplined for something, that they thought was wrong. I guess I kept it from reaching the light of day for a couple of reasons. One reason was the childhood love that I still kept for my mother; secondly, I believed that my life would be full of pain from the discipline and anger of the Christian matrons and Daddy Joseph in the home.

I did but was never clear on the wrongness of it because my mother was the only blood relative I knew and I wanted to protect that connection, and for a few years, I often would find a place to be by myself and talk to my mother.

The fact that she never came to take me out of the rock walls of the home for some good feeling of attachment to someone real in my family tree began to wear on my spirit. I began to look to my insides for strength and was substituting my feelings for Mother with hate and distance, and the hurt began to go away from my daily life. I believe that what I did was to put the entire structure of that experience and the following neglect by my mother over the years into a box and place the box deep inside my soul. And as a file can be forgotten, that file was never privileged to have that luxury in my young life. I often wanted to tell someone; however, it was filed away until now. I often in my growing-up years wondered how much my experience with my mother affected my life. The experience of producing a climax was a thrilling and exciting feeling inside my body.

As I continued to have periods of loneliness due to the deprivation of being loved by someone who would love me for me and as I am,

I longed for a relationship that others had with their parents who came to pick them up for the weekends. To fill those hours and pains of loneliness, I found a good feeling in giving myself a climax. And though I was told how wrong it was to turn to yourself to supply this good feeling, I nevertheless found it to be a panacea for those moments of aloneness.

Even though I thought about girls, I was not able to think about trying to get close enough to a girl to say or do anything that could be construed as being fresh or wanting more from them in the way of necking, etc., I was lost for something this romantic. I don't know of how it might have affected my later years above twenty, but I do know it became an option as opposed to going through the process of finding and having sex with a woman. A couple of the boys had pictures from some magazine that were shown to me, but for some reason, they weren't real to me, and I never got excited about them at all. I was just too bashful for that, so I used the self-fulfilling act of masturbation to take the heat off of my conscious self. I stopped this exercise by fourteen years of age.

There was an older boy who came to the home for a short time, Bob Donald. His grandmother would take him out on the weekends, and she let him take her car out for drives around town.

Bob had no money for gas, so he hit on an idea to siphon gas out of the home's bus. I had no idea about how to do this, but he showed me how to do this, even though the first time I swallowed gas and liked to die from coughing up. The home's yellow bus always parked next to Delila's cabin next to the kitchen area next to the alley.

There was a gate into the alley behind the bus, and Bob would bring his grandmother's car up next to the gate, and we would proceed to siphon the gas out of the bus for his car. My reward was that I got to go for a ride downtown and back. It didn't take long, but it was fun.

When Bob left the home, my siphoning expertise left with him. A few years later, I heard from Bob in California and went to see him at his company that was into waste management. Decades later, I got a call from him from Redding, or Red Bluff, in that area for sure. Bob bought eighteen hundred acres of land in that area and built a down-the-road children's home for boys. This was to be a Christian home for boys in California.

Bob wanted me to join him, but I was married to my present wife, Linda, at the time and could not accommodate him. Bob certainly put his short time in the home to good use years later.

It was about this time in my home life that I, at the ripe old age of thirteen, decided to run away from the home. I left and went up Cheyenne Boulevard to 21st Street and then over to Colorado City. From Colorado City I went west to Manitou. I ended up in the Penny Arcade watching the other kids play the games on the many machines. When they were going to close the arcade, I found a place to hide away for the night. I was getting hungry, but with no money, I just slept the night until the police picked me up the next morning and back to the home I went.

I was glad to get something to eat, and the punishment didn't hurt so much as the matron hit my legs just four time. And the sting lasted a short time when it competed with the joy of eating again.

I remember one night around 2:00 a.m., I was coming back from the restroom when I looked out the window and saw what looked like a fire in the main building where the girls lived. I woke Uncle Todd and Aunt Janet up. We went over to the building, and the kitchen area was on fire and was moving pretty fast. Aunt Janet called the fire department. Uncle Todd and I went upstairs and began waking up all the girls, and we actually carried out some of the small girls, and I carried out Pamela Stedly last from the big girls' dorm. I was fourteen and a bit husky, so Uncle Todd had me carry out some of the bigger girls. Pamela was a bit shorter but somewhat lighter than I, so it worked out all right.

They repaired the kitchen and pantry area the following week. We didn't miss a meal, however. That was quite a fire, an experience I won't forget.

The Christian doctrine was very rigid in its moral code controls, as taught to us by the home, that we were way too naive and bashful to explore anything but handholding. I guess that I began to think about the desires to kiss a girl in the ninth grade. I liked Wynona very much, but she was so nice I couldn't think of anything, but maybe getting a kiss from her somewhere down the road.

I don't think I was good looking, I was a freckled-faced, red-haired boy who was a bit on the chunky side. No one thought that I was a good-looking boy. At least, that was my impression. I also knew that being from the home did not set too well with the girls outside of the home. I believe this was why the girls in the home were so attracted to boys from elsewhere than the home. Many of the boys from town had cars that impressed the girls at the home.

I must confess there were two girls that befriended me and treated me special. I just did not have the courage to try and go with them even though I felt I had a chance. I could not even take them any place like a date—how boring I must have been to those who may have taken a liking to me. They were also blonds in the ninth grade at the junior high. Nothing ever came of that—nothing could, for sure.

I learned how to play basketball at the Boys Club of Colorado Springs. Uncle Todd recognized that I had athletic talent. He would violate the home policy and give me a quarter to go up to the club in the evening and play with the local boys. One boy, Joseph Booker, spent a lot of time with me and always picked me to play on his team.

My school mate was Jesse Pell. Her older brother was a Golden Gloves Champion, His name was Oliver Pell, or as he was called by friends, Oli Pell. Jesse was trained by her brother to defend herself. One day after school and before the home's bus came to pick me up, four Mexican boys from the valley were cornering me on the west side of the building. Jesse came out and said, "I will cover your back, Spud." We proceeded to clean house, and I thanked her for her help. Apparently, the guys were upset at being beaten in speedball that day at noon.

I never forgot that experience and the friendship we established. I was crossing South Colorado Boulevard in Denver on one of my working trips years later, and who should I see crossing the street in front of me, none other than my friend Jesse Pell. I called to her and since she was off work at Writers' Manor in Denver, I took her to lunch. What a thrill to see her crossing in front of me at a stoplight, and what a nice person Jesse was in my life.

We had the opportunity to try out for the high school varsity team. Joe and I made it and later lettered in the sport at the high school. The coach, Coach Morris, was so proud of both of us.

## IT WASN'T MEANT TO BE

Just before we were to play in the Christmas Tournament, Uncle Todd came to the high school gym and said I had to quit basketball. Uncle Todd was sad but said that I had to leave the home and would not be back to school. Daddy Joseph had me sent to Colorado Community Hospital in Denver for psychiatric evaluation. I was never told, even when I asked in later years, what the problem was with me at the home. Their explanation was that I was incorrigible and was a bad influence on the other kids. Dr. Dodd was my doctor at Colorado Community Hospital, and when he talked with me, he told me that for my health, he and the hospital felt it was important to keep me away from the strict, religious home for a while. They also said I was too interested in sex for my age.

It ended up being two months and I never received any treatments but a conversation with Dr. Dodd was very clear in telling me that he wanted to keep me away from the rigid, religious controls of the home. He said he believed the home was too interested in their religion to properly care for me. The hospital involved me in all kinds of games, and I had my own room, which kept me away from others in Ward D. I didn't take up smoking; however, I learned a few swear words and heard a lot of dirty jokes. Funny, everything that I was in there for never came up, but it became a school for adult languages and jokes. I learned some fine traits as well. One of these traits was to make leather belts, etc. in the leather shop.

The Doctor and the nurses—Joan Delaware, Betty Kinellson, and a good-looking redhead—gave a lot of attention and value to the differences between sexes and the bridge which brought the two together. I loved these nurses, and for different reasons. Joan seemed older and more mature. Betty was a wild personality and exciting, and the redhead was the youngest, perhaps a student, who was really nice to this young man, even to the extent she would drop by during her off-work hours. She was a beautiful young woman.

I used to spend a lot of time with a man who was dying. He died a week later from cancer in the lungs. We wrote a poem that was about smoking called the "Cigarette". I was fifteen, and it left an impression on this young mind. The man was responsible for most of the input. I wrote this in my little notebook in 1949, and I still have that old little notebook.

One other older man had figured a way to get out of the hospital. He wanted to know if I would like to go with him. I agreed to go because I could go find Joan and, maybe, Betty.

Anyway, we took sheets from his bed, unscrewed the window covers—a metal screen—and tied the two sheets together and put them out the window late at night. I went down first and made it safely. Bill started coming down the sheets. His weight was too much, and halfway down, the sheets broke, and he fell the rest of the way and was hurt but not discouraged. I was laughing at Bill's fall, and he did get upset with me. We took off, I said goodbye to Bill, and he disappeared into the night. I never saw Bill again and don't know what happened to him after that fall.

I knew that Joan worked at General Hospital, so I worked my way down town to where the hospital was. I found Joan, and was she surprised to see me. First, she thought that I had been released. I told her the story and she took time off to sell me on the idea of going back to the hospital. She took me back that very night. I had big wet tears rolling down my cheeks. I was so happy to see her. She was such a nice person. Dr. Dodd was surprised but not with my desire to get out of the hospital. He made arrangements for me to go to the Bylons Home for Boys. Incidentally, this home no longer exists.

I tried to backtrack my life through these homes and found out that several of them had no records for me to have concerning my life. I was sad that Joan said good-bye, and I never saw or heard from her again even though I tried to find her when I finally left the Lord's Home For Children.

The Bylons Home for boys was probably a good home, but I was so homesick for the friends at the old home and Wynona that I became a problem for the new home. I went to South High School, but I felt like fish out of water.

The folks in the home contacted the Lord's Home, and after they agreed to take me back, I was sent back to the home, much to my excitement. Uncle Todd and Aunt Janet were happy to see me.

I was getting excited about going to the high school in fall, because I would get to play basketball with my old playmates from the old junior varsity basketball team at this high school. I was enrolled into the Colorado Springs High School in fall. I began working out every afternoon with the basketball team under Coach Morris. My junior varsity coach was George Trump. He was one of the most noted football coaches in Colorado! He never had a losing season in sixteen years—some record I'd say.

I went out for football but the home wouldn't let me. It was a dangerous sport. Uncle Todd convinced Daddy Joseph that I was a quality basketball player, and it would help keep me occupied and challenged in school. Lastly, Daddy Joseph once told me I was the worst kid he had in the home and though I did a lot of childish things wrong, Uncle Todd was the only person who recognized that and supported me as much as he could within the boundaries of Daddy Joseph's rules.

I mentioned this before, but my mother plays on the back roads of my mind so often. I would love to have been able to tell someone about my mother, but I knew if I did, I would never get to see her again. And as I said earlier, I loved my mother, and in spite of what had happened, was the only living human being that came to take me out because I was her son. And it felt so good to be going out the gate with her because I was a part of her. I became bitter about my mother as I grew older. It was wrong—what she did was terribly wrong.

What happened had nothing to do with me. I was a mischievous boy with a lot of talent in and out of school. It would be better for me if I could live within the boundaries of Daddy Joseph's rules.

In my reentry into the Lord's Home for Children at fifteen years of age, having been in the Bylons Home for Boys as well as the Colorado Community Hospital, I brought with me a new-learned skills—i.e., playing poker, pool, smoking cigarettes, using curse words, and a portfolio of dirty jokes, even though I did not smoke.

Although I never took up the habit there, I did get to taste a cigarette or two. These were the contribution of the stay at the hospital for two months. Oh, I also learned to make leather belts and had a new appreciation for older girls, i.e., the beautiful caring student nurses.

It was during this time that a girl came to visit the home with her grandmother. Her grandmother brought on a trip to Colorado Springs to visit the home of Daddy Joseph's family. The girl had just graduated from high school in Panonia, Texas.

She and I hit it off as friends, and she was certainly a pretty woman. We talked about kissing one day, and she was surprised that I hadn't been kissed. Her name was Vera Dungess, and she gave me one big long kiss. I was fifteen at the time. They left the next day, and when I was later in the Marine Corps, I looked her up. I never forget that kiss.

I went to Padonia, Texas, and met her. She was engaged to be married, so we spent a short time together outside of town in a small parkway of the highway. I often wondered how she got along in life, but her kiss certainly set the stage for a better performance by me later in life from that time on. I got a good –bye kiss when I left.

I am not sure how many tricks were in my bag of information, but I am certain a few came rolling out on the table of life. I did find out that the reason they sent me for the evaluation was that I was taking an interest in sex too young and I had become very unmanageable or, using their word, incorrigible.

I wonder if this might have been a ruse to be used as a cover-up due to their inability to meld their very strict biblical interpretation with the normalcy of growing boys under their supervision. In any case, it was masked over to allow the execution of their decision in God's name.

In either case, they got back more than they sent away in the world of benefits, and in return, for their decision to achieve them with the incarceration of a fifteen-year-old boy.

The last belt whipping I received at the home was from Uncle Todd's razor strap. I at breakfast had put salt in Miss Duggen's sugar bowl for her tea. That got me my last whipping from Uncle Todd. He said later that he was afraid I was going to fight him at that time, but that was never a thought for I knew he had to do it as an example for those I would leave behind. I loved Uncle Todd and Aunt Janet. I made the varsity team and was set to go to a Christmas Tournament in Denver, and all of a sudden, I was taken home. Uncle Todd told me that the home made a decision to send me away from the home—or kick me out, is a better word for it.

# CHAPTER SEVEN

## ON MY OWN

For the second time, they made me leave what I really loved, basketball, and go out into the streets. I wanted to hate them, but remembering the good doctors' advice, I knew it was Daddy Joseph's sole decision, based upon some religious principle.

Uncle Todd and Aunt Janet had tears in their eyes as they told me of the decision by Daddy Joseph.

They were to give me three dollars for the bus to get to town and give me a bag of the clothes I was wearing and that were in my locker. I pleaded with them but to no avail. They let me go to school and tell the coach that I had to quit school and go to work. The coach had tears in his eyes as he told me he was so sorry for I had a promising position on the team and was a good player.

I used to shoot ten shots from the outside circle with the coach after practice, and we would shoot for a Coke. I used to beat him, but never wanted to collect from him. I said I had to go for the home's bus was waiting for me outside of the gym. I was gushing with tears when I reached Uncle Todd in the bus to go home.

The pain from not going with the team on a four-day weekend tournament just kept me crying all the way home on the bus.

That Christmas Tournament was the biggest event to come my way in so many years, but it was not to be. The home never told me why I was kicked out of the home, and Uncle Todd wouldn't say anything about it to me.

He just said that Daddy Joseph had made the decision to send me on my way. I never understood why this happened. The papers that would be valuable to me were not allowed to get into my hands.

I packed all of my clothes in an old suitcase that Uncle Todd dug up in the home attic on third floor. Uncle Todd gave me three dollars to take a bus to town, which was two miles away.

I walked uptown rather than use three dollars he gave me. I continued to ask Uncle Todd why the home was kicking me out.

I was sixteen now and thought I was doing fine at the home. They never gave me an answer, and for years, I asked for one. The home would not let me see any of my records. I guess they were pretty bad. In the state of Colorado, the homes, apparently were not required to provide the information to the child upon request.

I walked the two miles to town instead of spend the money on the bus. Plus, I knew I would have to eat. I ran into the man who owned the shoe repair shop where I earlier learned to shine shoes for pay. He advised me to go to the unemployment department uptown. The folks at the unemployment office said they had a job for me starting the next morning at the Blue Rock Bottling Company, which was in Manitou. The lady asked me if I had a place to sleep, and of course, I said no. She told me to take the receipt to the Welton Hotel and tell the clerk I had job starting on Wednesday and would pay them when I got paid.

The job started the day before Christmas. They gave me a room. I put my things in the room and went across the street to Bart's Ice Cream place. After having a chocolate shake, I went back to the Welton. I asked the clerk about some transportation options to Manitou. She advised me that at 7:00 a.m. for thirty cents one way, I could catch a bus.

When I got to town, Uncle Todd did tell me to go to the unemployment office to find work. They gave me a certificate stating I had a job starting Monday, just before Christmas Day. My job consisted of taking the cases that had been filled with quart-sized bottles and stack them on a skid seven levels up. It was tough getting the cases up to the sixth and seventh levels, but I was a husky little guy with a survival determination and no money to eat on.

After a few weeks, Duke the Irishman promoted me to inspector of the bottles on the moving rack. I got to look through a magnifying glass twelve inches across to look for obvious impurities in the bottles as they came off the line. The fella's at work told me that Duke had a steel plate in his head. They think that is what made him ornery.

I took the bus every morning at seven o'clock and arrived at the company at 7:45. I got to go home at, five o'clock. Duke used to keep us going with a big boot in the butt, and he was so big that the boot lifted me off of the ground.

He only had to do that one time to me. I was a quick learner, you see.

I stretched the three dollars Uncle Todd gave me mostly eating fatty food for my consumption and tastes.

When I got back to the Welton Hotel, I took a shower and felt better. I would go over to Bart's Ice Cream Store across the street and get another chocolate. I walked around downtown for a while and then went home to get some sleep.

I was tired after a day at work. I was sitting downstairs in the lobby talking to the clerk when an older man sat down and joined the conversation. The topic got to food, and the man saw that I was really hungry. He said his name was George, and that he was going out for some dinner and asked if I would like to come along. I thought he was staying the Welton, so I felt safe and comfortable eating with him, especially since he said he was buying. We went out to a place that makes hamburgers. I can't remember the name of the place down by the courthouse on Nevada.

After we ate, and I did get full, we started walking back to the Welton. He asked about my background and told me he was visiting from Denver on business. We sat down stairs for a while and then I told him I had to go upstairs and get to bed. George said he was going up as well and wondered if he might join me for a little while. I thought this guy fed me, and the least I could do was let him come up to talk for a while.

We talked about sports, and then I told him I had to go to bed. He said he would leave as soon as I got into bed. I guess I felt obligated to be nice to him since he treated me to dinner. I felt a little uncomfortable because I slept in the nude because I didn't have anything to wear other than my work clothes.

I scooted into bed and threw the covers over me. George said he was a workout trainer and that I'm pretty muscular and wondered if he could just feel my leg muscles and then he would leave. I didn't see anything wrong with that. I guess I was a bit flattered, so I said yes. After all, the man did just buy me dinner.

He began to feel my leg muscles, and he eventually got to my groin. By then he had gotten me sexually excited, and he played with my penis with his mouth until I reached a climax. It felt temporarily good, but I felt embarrassed and hurt. And as I turned over under my covers, I told him to leave and never come back. I had now become angry and stupid and hurt.

Thanks to the home and its religious teachings, I was certainly naïve and was open prey for a person like him. I fought it within my mind and heart for some time and was so sorry I was so stupid at sixteen years of age. I have never told a soul about this experience. It would be too embarrassing and hurtful to me.

Looking back, I believed I owed him something out of gratitude for buying me dinner. I was hoping he never come around anymore and eventually put it behind me as a learning experience. I worked at the bottling company through July 1950.

I shall always remember my first money that didn't go for the Welton Hotel weekly fee. With the first discretionary funds I had, I bought a little Victrola to play records on. I bought some old, classic records that the store said came with it. I enjoyed so much listening to those classics at night before I turned out the lights.

One of the guys I worked with said his little brother was parking cars at the Pine Valley Country Club up north of town. He put me in contact with his brother, Joseph, and I started going out to the country club with Joe. We made good money on tips. Joe was eighteen, and when we finished at night we came back to the hotel and divided the money.

I did this for three nights, and my take was about thirty to thirty-five dollars a night. I only worked on Friday, Saturday, and Sunday nights. The clerk saw us sitting at a table in the lobby dividing our money, and he believed we might be stealing the money. Well, the Police came and questioned us, and when they found that I didn't have a driver's license and my age, I was ordered to stop, which I did.

## UNITED STATES MARINE CORPS

A guy I worked with said that I should look into joining the service—good pay, room and board, and girls were more readily available to the guys in the service. I checked and found that I had to be seventeen years of age with my parents consent. I looked over my choices and believed that the Marine Corps would be the best. I honestly felt that if I am going to war, I would rather be with the toughest service and the one considered the best.

I went to the marines and talked with them and said I had to have a parent sign for me. I told them about my past and they steadfastly said I needed a parent's signature. I faced a dilemma in that my mother was the only living parent, and I had no idea where she was located. I knew she was a registered nurse, and she took me with her to the Will Brady Hospital for the mentally insane or very sick. I went to the hospital and they could not help me for she had left the hospital years before. I decided to go to Cheyenne and see if I could find her and that old fella she was living with at the hotel. The old man had died, and no one knew a thing about my mom.

I visited several Denver hospitals and found that she had, indeed, worked for some of them; however, when I tried to get more information from them they were closemouthed about her.

I found out from one of them that she was fired, and when I ask why, the clerk said in a whisper that she was caught in bed with working members of the hospitals as well as with some of the patients. The clerk, again in a whisper, said she was considered a nymphomaniac. I guess that may explain why she had the affair with me at thirteen.

I gave up looking for her in Denver and decided to catch a bus home to Colorado Springs and give up any idea of joining the Marine Corps until I was eighteen years of age.

As I was going into that big and busy bus station on Broadway in Denver, I ran into a woman in the doorway of the depot. As I passed the lady, I bumped into her in the doorway. I heard her say, "Bobby, is that you?" I turned to look, and sure enough, it was my mother. I said, "Mom," and she gave me a hug. And her perfume hadn't changed in all of these years.

I was both happy and sad, but more happy than sad, still with a bit of anger in my heart. I told her of my plight, and that I needed her signature to go into the marines.

My mother said she would sign for me if I would make sure to sign my ten-thousand-dollar life insurance policy with her as the beneficiary—the insurance I will have when I join the marines. She made this a requirement for her signature, and this again made me angry inside. I wanted her signature, so I agreed with her requirement. We went up to the recruiter's office, and he signed me up and put her name on as the beneficiary of my insurance.

The recruiter told me that I could change the beneficiary at any time after I get active. He said this to me after she left and was waiting in the hall. We parted at the bus depot and I went home to Colorado Springs. I don't know where she was headed.

Even though the religious homes were strict, we learned how to live with other people. We were regimented in mind. We did get some kind of work ethic in the home, and we didn't get involved in the drinking and smoking world around us. We could take instructions from the matrons, who now were replaced with the drill instructors that took over where the matrons left off. This transfer of authority kept boys like me a bit ahead of the crowd.

I left so many bad experiences behind and became a marine through and through. I learned long ago that for every infraction of the rules, there was an equal reaction by authority. Knowing that for an action there was always an equal and direct reaction,

I came away from the home life with a deep sense of faith in God, and it has been a lighthouse in the world into which I am going. Coming from a home of regimentation was a plus for the Marine Corps—government-issued food, etc. We were already prepared for the Marines corp.

Many of the kids coming out of these places come out with one of two attitudes. They either believe the world owes them something or they owe the world something for the years they spent in the homes. I believed I owed the world something, and with the philosophy that I believed every person had a private world of their own, in which they found satisfaction and self-assurance of their value as a person.

People became my asset in life and they were my value. This has helped me do well handling people in life. Unfortunately, my preoccupation with humans as the most important asset I had seemed to keep me not having the dollar as my objective.

I believed every person had a private world that should be respected and not violated unless they gave you permission. Unfortunately, this kept me from trying to get closer to women I thought were well worth loving.

I wanted first to become friends before I became romantically involved. This is probably the reason it took me so long to ask for permission to kiss the woman to whom, I had grown very fond. I guess as some friends called me square, I really was at this time.

It is interesting to note that after I was teaching in Mountain High School for a few years, that Daddy Joseph asked me to come back to the home and be the new superintendent. I told him I could not run the home that was not child oriented but religion oriented. He thanked me for my honesty, and we parted still friends.

# REFERENCES

Sally Abrahms, "3 Generations Under One Roof," *AARP* (2013). http://www.aarp.org/home-family/friends-family/info-04-2013/three-generations-household-american-family.html.

_Sord Holdren_
719 – 368 – 6222

CPSIA information can be obtained
at www.ICGtesting.com
Printed in the USA
FFHW020012300119
50320200-55450FF

9 781499 067637